VIETNAM BUSINESS GUIDE

Getting Started in Tomorrow's Market Today

VIETNAM BUSINESS GUIDE

Getting Started in Tomorrow's Market Today

Brian and Kimberly Vierra

WILEY

John Wiley & Sons (Asia) Pte. Ltd.

Other Wiley Editorial Offices

John Wiley & Sons, 111 River Street, Hoboken, NJ07030, USA
John Wiley & Sons, The Atrium, Southern Gate, Chichester, West Sussex, PO19 8SQ,
    United Kingdom
John Wiley & Sons (Canada) Ltd., 5353 Dundas Street West, Suite 400, Toronto,
    Ontario, M9B 6HB, Canada
John Wiley & Sons Australia Ltd, 42 McDougall Street, Milton, Queensland 4064,
    Australia
Wiley-VCH, Boschstrasse 12, D-69469 Weinheim, Germany

Library of Congress Cataloging-in-Publication Data

ISBN 978-0-470-82452-8

Typeset in 10/13.5 Quorum Book by Aptara Inc., New Delhi, India
Printed in Singapore by International Press Softcom Limited
10 9 8 7 6 5 4 3 2 1

Contents

Preface

On a warm evening in November of 2000, we were walking along a beach in the Dominican Republic, reflecting on the great day we had just had. We had spent most of the morning mountain biking through the hills with an adventure sports operator that ran a variety of trips in the country. In a contemplative moment I thought out loud, "I bet we could run a trip like what we did today. I've traveled to lots of great places where this would work. I bet we could even do it better." And thus our first business was born.

At that time Kim was working in New York City as a human resources consultant and I was an import manager for a global logistics company. We had met in an international business master's program in Portland, Oregon, two years previous to this, and were dutifully applying what we had learned and walking the path that many business managers before us had trodden; climbing the corporate ladder and angling for the next promotion.

It wasn't that we were unhappy in our jobs. Kim loved the kind of work she was doing in New York and today works for the same employer in Singapore. I had just been promoted and was working on a number of interesting projects. But we wanted to create something that was our own; take what we loved to do, find a way to turn it into a business, and make a living out of it. We are avid outdoors people, so we wanted to turn what we were doing on the weekend into a job that we could do every day.

Once we had committed to the idea of pursuing a business of our own, we needed to find a suitable location. Our master's degrees were in international business with a focus on Asia, but neither of us had any experience in trying to run an adventure business. So we decided to narrow our search in Asia to those countries where we would encounter very little competition; we wanted time to learn how to make our business work without getting into an immediate slugfest with established operators. The more we researched, the more we realized that we were going to have to forge into one of the lesser-developed Southeast Asian countries where our business model would be unique and the competition limited, or at best non-existent. We also wanted to base ourselves where the weather is conducive to year-round activities. Deciding to set up our company in Vietnam, therefore, was the logical conclusion, and, in November 2001, after a year of working on a business plan and feasibility study, we set off on our Vietnam adventure.

It was probably better that we had no idea of what we were getting into. Vietnam had very recently opened its doors to foreign investment and was beginning to recover from the Asian Financial Crisis of 1997. There were few books about doing business in Vietnam. There were very few people who could advise us on how to set up a private business. In fact, Vietnam had just made it legal for private Vietnamese businesses to exist in 2000—the year before we arrived.

Undaunted, we spent a couple of months traveling throughout the country searching for a suitable location. After dismissing several of our previous location ideas, we stumbled upon a beautiful, old hill town in the central highlands, a colonial retreat where the French escaped the heat of Saigon back when Vietnam was a part of French Indochina. The climate was temperate, and traveling out into the hills on our mountain bikes we found an abundance of natural places to explore and a small town, alive with adventure possibilities. We fell in love with the place. But this is where the easy part of our plan ended.

Although we initially spoke with lawyers in Ho Chi Minh City about setting up a business in Vietnam, we decided to pursue the task on our own. We thought that our independent natures and intense curiosity would help us navigate the path we had chosen. In reality the experience was exhausting, frustrating and bewildering. The only thing that kept us going was having no idea how much more we would have to go through. From the massive amount of documentation required for licensing to the ambiguity of what our responsibilities would be, the process of making our business legal nearly got the better of us. Still, we refused to give up simply because we had already come so far. Eventually, in November 2001 our company was established. We could finally experience the joy of working in a business that was our very own.

In 2003, we created our second business; a corporate training company addressing the training needs of multinational firms operating in Vietnam. This time we used a lawyer. The process was still frustrating, but with the compass of our previous experience, and with the help of a good lawyer things were more expeditious and less confusing.

Fast forward to 2009. We had gained valuable knowledge with our hands-on approach—from the licensing of our business to the intricacies of the tax regime and labor contracts—but we had also learned that it's better to get help. After such a long and interesting journey, we decided our experiences and insights should be passed on to others, which is why we've written this book.

Vietnam is a beautiful country that is developing quickly and offers a plethora of opportunities to the bold and adventurous business person. An adventure is guaranteed to all who seek business opportunities here, but going in with a good understanding of what to expect will increase the chance for success. We hope our book serves as a guide to avoiding pitfalls and surmounting obstacles. Most importantly we hope to help entrepreneurs enter into the modern and rapidly-evolving Vietnamese business world.

Special thanks are due to all those who helped make this book possible. To our publisher John Wiley and Sons and especially CJ Hwu. To our editor and friend, Mary Murakami. To all of those who took the time to speak to us about their experiences in Vietnam and act as the experts on different topics including Vu Minh Tri, Aidan Lynam, Chad Ovel, Luzius Wipf, Seth Restaino, and Amanda Tucker. To ORC Worldwide, for generous contributions to the Living in Vietnam section. To our parents, who said "You're quitting your jobs, moving to Vietnam and doing what?" and then fully supported us anyway. And finally to the many others who took the time to speak with us and chose to remain anonymous. We thank you all.

Introduction

"When the prison doors are opened, the dragon will fly out."

Ho Chi Minh

The battle still rages on in Vietnam, although the theatre of operations is different. It's a true fight to succeed in the Vietnamese business environment. The opportunities of a populous and quickly developing country lure many a naïve investor into what inevitably proves too grueling an experience to overcome. The big multinationals have the resources, lawyers and accountants to capitalize on the opportunities, but even they suffer casualties. While a particular project may not fail, many expatriates, brought in as country managers and paid top dollar, do.

Simply applying the strategies that have worked for a company elsewhere in Asia could prove fatal in Vietnam. The culture and history of the country have sculpted a workforce and workplace unlike anything else seen in Asia. Most readers are familiar with a brief history of the country through the Vietnam War (called the American War in Vietnam), and have seen Hollywood's inter-pretations. It's critical to know that the conflict ended fairly recently (1975), and the Vietnamese people that you want to work with are very much a product of their country's history. Vietnam is still a communist country, and one that is just emerging from a long period of isolation and an even longer period of war. Capitalism is in its infant stages.

In the Heritage Foundation's 2009 Index of Economic Freedom, Vietnam was ranked 145th of 179 countries. Hong Kong and Singapore, by comparison, rank first and second. Using this index as a measure of the ease of conducting business, one could say that it would be easier to choose to conduct business in Hong Kong, Singapore, and 142 other countries of the world, rather than conducting it in Vietnam.

Nevertheless, there are good reasons to be interested in doing business in Vietnam. With the past decade of growth at over 7.5 percent, the country of 85 million people has transformed itself from a nation that could barely feed itself into a major exporter of agricultural produce. Vietnam has become a huge exporter of textiles and furniture, and in 2007 produced more shoes for Nike than any other country. With companies like Intel investing upwards of $1 billion, electronics manufacturing is poised for rapid growth. Workers' wages are still lower than in other competing countries like China and worker productivity is increasing.

While there are reasons to be optimistic about business prospects in Vietnam, there are an equally good number of reasons to be cautious. The country experienced one mass exodus of investors in the late 1990s during the Asian Financial Crisis. An important consideration is that inflation as of July 2008 was an annualized rate of 25 percent, and the cost of doing business is rising rapidly. Several companies have recently endured strikes at factories because workers' paychecks aren't meeting the rising cost of living. What other countries view as corruption is still accepted business practice in Vietnam. In addition to these macro economic factors that one will encounter when entering Vietnam, there are a host of cultural barriers to success.

We've done our best to give you a roadmap to guide you through the intricacies of the Vietnamese business landscape as it exists today. Unfortunately, the "roads" are being altered on a monumental scale and at a very rapid pace. In light of Vietnam's history, it is important to take our information about where to go and what to do, as well as the current laws and procedures, as a starting point to your very own adventure. Change happens fast in Vietnam, which is what makes doing business, and writing about doing business, so exciting and at the same time so challenging.

This book was written from 2008 into early 2009, and while the country was focusing all of its energy on growth and was increasing foreign domestic investment to astronomical new heights, insidious inflation crept in the back door. Vietnam's leaders quickly changed from the growth strategy that had served them so well, to a strategy focused on cooling the country's inflationary state. What happens next in Vietnam, whether fortune or misfortune, is up to the global economy, the government, the people, and the companies operating there.

STRUCTURE OF THE BOOK

Part 1: Considering Vietnam—Get Ready!

Doi moi, or "renovation," was launched by the Sixth Party Congress in 1986. Foreign entrepreneurs rushed in to enjoy the low–wage labor and to be first to present their products and services to the brand-conscious Saigonese. Many of these early pioneers, however, realized that low wages and an eager workforce weren't enough to keep their investments in-country; they also needed consistent investment-friendly financial policies and a solid legal system.

With Vietnam's accession into the World Trade Organization (WTO) in 2007, most of these companies are back again for a second try, along with a crowd of new companies who are entering fiercely competitive markets against already entrenched players in a country that is still experiencing major reforms. Vietnam's critics claim that the *doi moi* door that slammed shut on some eager faces in the early 90s will most likely swing shut again, but Vietnam's enthusiasts are betting that the WTO will be able to wedge the door open permanently.

Thus, it is important to discover if you and your company's production needs, products or services are right for Vietnam and to decide if Vietnam is right for you. Part 1 of our book highlights the opportunities and the threats to your success.

It gives you information about Vietnam. Are you looking to manufacture in Vietnam and take advantage of the relatively cheap labor? Do you have a product or service that would market well to its population of over 85 million? Does Vietnam fit in well with a larger regional business initiative? We will explain the attracting forces that Vietnam is perceived to have and what is the reality.

Also covered in Part 1 are the trials and tribulations of life in Vietnam. If your company has asked you to take an assignment in Vietnam, please know that a happy family makes for a happy, productive expatriate. Has your spouse spent much time in the third world or in developing countries? Are you and your family comfortable outside of Western cultures and without familiar social amenities? Can you handle jam-packed roads and inefficient government processes? If you answered no to any of these questions, you must seriously consider whether Vietnam is the place for you.

Part 2: Starting up in Vietnam—Get Set!

The middle section of the book is dedicated to understanding the important details for setting up operations in Vietnam: from establishing your legal presence, securing a business address and hiring and training your employees.

Vietnam is an extremely bureaucratic environment. The licensing phase requires an enormous amount of documentation and the procedures seem very confusing. Knowing what to expect can help to alleviate some of the shock one might experience during the start-up phase of a business. A good understanding of the process can help foresee potential delays and set realistic timelines.

Many companies decide that they can't survive alone in Vietnam, so they look for a local partner. Business relationships in Vietnam are built upon trust—not contracts—and trust must be built up over time. It doesn't occur with a simple signature on the bottom of a contract. Westerners and Vietnamese have differing perceptions of contracts. In the West they are generally binding, while in Vietnam (and in other Asian countries), they are merely a guideline—the first step in a relationship, a flexible entity that evolves over time. The real contract is the quality of the relationship that is built to govern the business and its operations. What is said in everyday conversations is far more important than what is written in a "legally binding" contract.

One of the most challenging aspects of doing business in Vietnam, and one of the most crucial to your success, is building an effective team. The competition for talent is fierce, with new multinationals coming into the country all the time and a shallow pool of skilled labor.

Again, we ask questions to guide your thinking. What legal framework will facilitate your business goals in Vietnam? Where should you base yourself; Hanoi, Ho Chi Minh City or one of the numerous other towns and cities? Should you partner with a local company or try to go it alone? How do you go about recruiting Vietnamese talent? What do the Vietnamese look for in an employer and what attracts the best talent? How can you select the best candidate (most likely an expatriate) to run your office? Can you succeed in the Vietnamese business environment?

Part 3: The Daily Challenges—Go!

After reading this section of our book you'll be aware of the cultural and legal differences that make doing business in Vietnam difficult for foreigners. You'll be aware of on-going challenges of corruption and infringement of your intellectual property.

Western ethics won't do you any good when dealing with Vietnamese customs officials, or traffic police. Nor will they help you when confronted with the challenge of "expediting" the issuance of a license. In many cases you must either temporarily suspend your sense of ethics, or your business will remain stuck in limbo.

Think about this: McDonald's operates over 31,000 restaurants in over 119 countries on six continents. So, why isn't there a single McDonald's restaurant in this country of over 85 million citizens? We have found communism to mean "what is yours is mine." Don't be surprised, for example, if you open up a successful seafood restaurant named Crab 41, and one morning you wake up to find the store next door is now a new restaurant called Crab 41, and if your business is very successful, the shop around the corner and the one across the street have also adopted your name. Because of the widely accepted practice of copycatting successful brands, one of your biggest daily challenges will be protecting your intellectual property.

This section will also address other daily challenges that you will face, such as understanding and complying with your personal and business tax obligations and operating companies in popular industries, such as manufacturing, outsourcing, and agriculture. Selling into the Vietnamese market can be quite complex, so this section offers questions and considerations for sales and marketing.

VIETNAM

C H I N A

Sapa

Red River

Thai Nguyen

Hanoi★   ●Halong City
●Haiphong

L

V

I

GULF OF

TONKIN

Hainan
(CHINA)

A

●Vinh

KEY TO ELEVATION
Sea level to 500 ft. (0–152 m)
500 to 1,000 ft. (152–305 m)
1,000 to 2,500 ft. (305–762 m)
2,500 to 5,000 ft. (762–1,524 m)
Above 5,000 ft (1,524+ m)

O

Mekong River

Hue●

Danang

T H A I L A N D

S

T

●Quang Ngai

N

●Quy Nhon

A

C A M B O D I A

Dalat●   ●Nha Trang

M

●Ho Chi Minh City
(Saigon)

Tan An●

GULF OF   Can Tho●

THAILAND

SOUTH

CHINA

SEA

0   100 mi
0   100 km

Map courtesy of Frommer's Travel Guides

PART 1
Considering Vietnam— Get Ready!

CHAPTER 1

Why Vietnam?

A SNAPSHOT OF VIETNAM'S ECONOMY

GDP (2008): $89.98 billion.

Real growth rate (2008 est.): 6.2 percent.

Per capita income (2008): $1,024.

Inflation rate (May 2008): 25 percent.

External debt (2008): 29.8 percent of GDP, $21.8 billion.

Natural resources: Coal, crude oil, zinc, copper, silver, gold, manganese, iron.

Agriculture, forestry, and fisheries: (20.25 percent of GDP, 2007) Principal products—rice, maize, sweet potato, peanut, soy beans, cotton, coffee, cashews.

Cultivated land: 12.2 million hectares.

Land use: 21 percent arable; 28 percent forest and woodland; 51 percent other.

Industry and construction: (41.62 percent of GDP, 2007) Principal types—mining and quarrying, manufacturing, electricity, gas, water supply, cement, phosphate, and steel.

Services: (38.13 percent of GDP, 2007) Principal types—tourism, wholesale and retail, repair of vehicles and personal goods, hotel and restaurant, transport storage, telecommunications.

Trade (2007): Exports—$48.39 billion. Principal exports—crude oil, garments/textiles, footwear, fishery products, wood products, rice (second-largest exporter in world), sea products, coffee, rubber, handicrafts. Imports—$60.8 billion. Principal imports—machinery, oil and gas, garment materials, iron and steel, transport-related equipment.

Major export partners: U.S., EU, Japan, China, Singapore, Australia, Taiwan, and Germany.

Major import partners: China, Japan, Singapore, Taiwan, South Korea, Hong Kong, and Thailand.[1]

ECONOMIC OVERVIEW

Vietnam is the 13th most populous country in the world and it has tremendous potential for a growing role in the global economy. It may be a late bloomer compared to other Southeast Asian nations such as Singapore, but the country seems destined for a positive future. Vietnam's GDP numbers are climbing at a record pace and much of this growth has been, and will most likely continue to be, due to the increasing levels of foreign investment. However, Vietnam seems to have a love-hate relationship with foreigners. Given its history of invasions (and some might say exploitations) by outside entities usually followed by fighting and then isolation, there is a warm welcome for invested funds but not necessarily the company/management that brings in the investment. There is an undercurrent of skepticism in many an investor, given the relatively insular nature of Vietnam in recent history, as well as Vietnam's philosophical reasoning for past isolation. Gaining trust is tricky for both parties. Foreigners want to trust that the historic cycles of boom and bust, of open and closed, have changed, and that the country will not choose to segregate itself from the international community again, while the government of Vietnam wants foreign cooperation without exploitation. These sometimes competing desires make for interesting government and industry interactions, as well as for potential misunderstandings and misinterpretations for both industry and government. Despite the following upbeat report from *The World Factbook*, there is still much work to be done in creating an inviting atmosphere for investors.

World Trade Organization (WTO) membership has provided Vietnam an anchor to the global market and reinforced the domestic economic reform process. Among other benefits, accession allows Vietnam to take advantage of the phase-out of the Agreement on Textiles and Clothing, which eliminated quotas on textiles and clothing for WTO partners on January 1, 2005. Agriculture's share of economic output has continued to shrink, from about 25 percent in 2000 to less than 20 percent in 2007. Deep poverty, defined as a percent of the population living under $1 per day, has declined significantly and is now smaller than that of China, India, and the Philippines. Vietnam is working to create jobs to meet the challenge of a labor force that is growing by more than one-and-a-half million people every year. In an effort to stem high inflation which took off in 2007, early in 2008 Vietnamese authorities began to raise benchmark interest rates and reserve requirements. Hanoi is targeting an economic growth rate of 7.5-8 percent during the next four years.[2]

According to the Heritage Foundation, which tracks economic freedom around the world:

Vietnam's economy is 49.8 percent free, according to our 2008 assessment, which makes it the world's 135th freest economy. Its overall score is 0.4 percentage point better than last year, mainly reflecting an improvement in trade freedom. Vietnam is ranked 25th out of 30 countries in the Asia–Pacific region, and its overall score is lower than the regional average.

In terms of size of government, Vietnam is above the world average. Government fiscal expenditures equal about one fourth of its GDP, which is relatively low comparatively speaking. Tellingly though, this statistic is limited in its utility. Weaknesses in Vietnam's government drive the low expenditure rate rather than bureaucratic efficiency. For a government that imposes relatively high personal tax rates, tax revenue is not accordingly high. This could be due to tax evasion, or due to lower-than-average personal income, or a combination of these factors.

Structurally, Vietnam has a weak record on financial freedoms, including investment, property rights and the freedom from governmental and private corruption. Although it is undergoing reform, the financial sector is neither well-regulated nor independent of the government. Despite some progress, foreign investment is subject to an array of opaque regulations and cannot be guaranteed legally. The judiciary is subject to political influence, and commercial cases often take years to reach resolution. Corruption is a serious problem in the legal system, as well as in the civil service as a whole. Various forms of corruption that affect foreign investors will be covered in depth throughout the book.

It is clear by looking at the numbers that many firms have decided, as illustrated in Table 1.1, the risks of entering Vietnam do not outweigh the rewards. In 2007, Vietnam attracted $21 billion in foreign direct investment (FDI), which was double the FDI amount in 2006, and as of mid-2008, was expected to attract $23 billion in the first half of the year. Foreign

Table 1.1   Top 10 sectors attracting foreign direct investment in Vietnam in 2007

Rank	Areas attracting Foreign Direct Investment	Percentage of Total Foreign Direct Investment
1	Manufacturing	45 percent
2	Construction of new apartments and buildings	26 percent
3	Hotel construction and other tourism-related projects	11 percent
4	Other construction	6 percent
5	Transport, post, telecom	3 percent
6	Industrial zone development	2 percent
7	Agribusiness including both agriculture and aquaculture (i.e. fisheries)	2 percent
8	Service sector	2 percent
9	New urban development	2 percent
10	Education, health and cultural	1 percent

Source: Ministry of Planning and Investment

direct investment into Vietnam is almost three times that of its behemoth northern neighbor, China, in per capita terms.

The areas that the Vietnam Ministry of Planning and Investment are most interested in increasing foreign direct investment into include:

1. Production of export goods;
2. Raising, farming and processing agricultural, forestry and aquatic products;
3. Investments involving high technology and know-how;
4. Environmental protection;
5. Research and development;
6. Labor-intensive industries;
7. The efficient use of raw materials and natural resources; and
8. Major infrastructure and production capacity projects.

Source: Department of Planning and Investment, Ho Chi Minh City

SUMMARY

For more details by industry, please reference Appendix A. The industries mentioned in the sector overview are not meant to be all-inclusive lists of available opportunities. Many other foreign businesses and investments in other industries have been successful in Vietnam including, for example, the hotel and tourism industry.

Regardless of your industry or product, it is critically important to research your optimal legal set-up and create a plan to protect yourself and your interests before entering Vietnam. Much space in this book is spent on these important points. While the opportunities available are exciting, Vietnam is a high-risk country. Remember that Vietnam is a developing economy and the systems critical to company protection such as the judiciary and financial systems have not yet completely developed. These economic and operational systems shortcomings contribute to Vietnam's higher-than-average risk factor.

WEB RESOURCES

Electricity of Vietnam Corporation (EVN): http://www.evn.com.vn

Ho Chi Minh City Computer Association: www.hca.org.vn

PetroVietnam: http://www.petrovietnam.com.vn/Modules/PVHome.asp

The Asian Development Bank: http://www.adb.org/VietNam/projects.asp

The World Bank: www.worldbank.org.vn

Vietnam Chamber of Commerce and Industry: http://vibforum.vcci.com.vn/

Vietnam Customs: http://www.customs.gov.vn/

Vietnam Economy: http://www.vneconomy.com.vn/eng/

Vietnam Internet Network Information Center (VNNIC): http://www.vnnic. net.vn

Vietnam Investment Review: http://www.vir.com.vn/Client/VIR/Default.asp

Vietnam Ministry of Industry and Trade (MoIT): http://www.moit.gov.vn

Vietnam's Ministry of Information and Communications (MIC): http://www. mic.gov.vn

Vietnam Ministry of Planning and Investment: http://www.mpi.gov.vn/

Vietnam Ministry of Science and Technology (MOST): http://www.most. gov.vn

Vietnam Post & Telecommunications Group (VNPT): http://www.vnpt.com.vn

Vietnam Ministry of Health: http://www.moh.gov.vn/homebyt/en/portal/ index.jsp

ENDNOTES

1. "Vietnam Background Notes," U.S. Department of State, http://www.state.gov/ r/pa/ei/bgn/4130.htm
2. *World Factbook: Vietnam*, U.S. Central Intelligence Agency, https://www.cia.gov/ library/publications/the-world-factbook/print/vm.html

CHAPTER 2
Living in Vietnam—It isn't for Everyone

With its accession into the World Trade Organization (WTO) in 2007, many companies are flocking to Vietnam to take advantage of the relatively low labor costs and make their mark in the second fastest growing economy in Asia, behind China. This movement has resulted in a significant increase in the number of available jobs, as shown in Table 2.1. Vietnam has a huge potential labor force, but there is a scarce supply of talent at middle management and executive levels. According to Winnie Lam of Navigos Group, an executive search firm in Vietnam, this situation has not only created an escalation in employee expectations, but also significantly impacts recruitment and retention practices. Employees have been expecting relatively high salaries, given their experience levels, and companies are doing everything they can to keep their employees happy, in order to prevent them from job hopping for incremental salary gains.

In this tight labor market, your company may not be able to find experienced, talented personnel locally and may join many others who send expatriates to Vietnam to fill the skills gap at the top and mid-level management positions.

Table 2.1 Vietnam's growing popularity – open positions indicator

Q1'07	Q2'07	Q3'07	Q4'07	Q1'08	Q2'08
10,550	15,025	15,964	17,647	20,647	20,712

Source: VietnamWorks

One Spouse's Story

She said that she had endured 245 days of "this ridiculous assignment to Vietnam" and had 485 to go. She lived for her annual home leave and said that she'd divorce her husband if he extended his contract for another year. She was misery personified.

As we pushed our kids on the playground swings of the swanky resort-style condominium where we lived, Jennifer told me her story. She was from South Carolina and had never been outside of the United States, except for one "super-fun!" trip to Mexico for spring break. She married her high school sweetheart and was the mother of their spirited two year-old boy when her husband got the call from his employer. Would he be interested in a liaison position in Vietnam to ensure that the company's furniture factories were consistently producing high quality pieces? The deal looked really good on paper—a big boost in pay, opportunity for a promotion and other tempting perks—but the deal didn't look so good to her anymore.

Since moving to Vietnam, she and her husband had had a second child with chronic health issues. They had enrolled their son in an international pre-school, and he was identified as having a learning disability, an assessment that she and her husband did not support. They suspected that the testing was motivated by the school's funding policy; the school receives $800 for each disability evaluation it performs. Additionally, her husband's travel to and from factories on dangerous roads took several hours each day which was stressful for both of them. Another difficulty was the company's expectation for him to wine and dine the factory management on a regular basis in order to maintain positive performance evaluations. He was highly stressed and she was lonely and frustrated.

Certainly, there are many wonderful aspects to life in Vietnam, including the ability to hire household staff, which is a luxury in many developed countries. Many expatriates enjoy a lower cost of living compared to their hometowns elsewhere; however, the challenges to daily living are many and some are severe.

What do expatriates experience living in Vietnam? When asked what he likes best about living there, VietnamWorks' director and expatriate, Jonah Levey said, "The food, the friendly people, and the real excitement of being a part of a rapidly developing economy."

On the downside, human resources professionals surveyed in ORC World-wide's 2006 Location-Specific Survey of International Assignment Policies and Practices say their foreign workforce in Vietnam cite disease, poor sanitation, and pollution as their main areas of concern. Other issues include insufficient medical facilities, the extreme climate, and a lack of familiar cultural, social, and recreational outlets. Companies will usually pay a premium to expatriate staff sent to Vietnam, to compensate for the unfavorable living conditions there. A recommendation for this hardship payment is available from ORC Worldwide.

If your company has asked you to take an assignment in Vietnam, and if you are married, remember this: a happy family makes for a happy, productive expatriate. Ask yourself if your spouse has spent much time in lesser developed countries? How will he or she react to strangers with dirty hands touching your child's face or hair? A gesture of friendship in Vietnam can cause anxiety for parents who are not familiar with Vietnamese conditions and customs.

Many expatriates underestimate the stress of living abroad. The decision to relocate internationally requires serious thought and deliberate preparation, even if there are exceptional opportunities to move up within your company or to start your own business. Because Vietnam is a developing economy with developing infrastructures such as medical facilities, families need to proceed very cautiously. Parents must be aware of (and prepared for) the unique hardships that can affect their children. While expatriate children can experience a different culture, and increase their world view during an international assignment, if they are at critical years in school, or have special needs, the move may be more stressful than beneficial. This would be the case for any international relocation, but the situation is exacerbated by the less-than-optimal living conditions in Vietnam. Appendix B contains more details on the living conditions in Vietnam that may affect you and/or your expatriated employees.

PART 2

Starting up in Vietnam—Get Set!

ROADMAP TO STARTING YOUR BUSINESS IN VIETNAM

Step	Action	Estimated cost to complete action	Estimated time to complete action
1	Obtain a business registration certificate from the local business registration office. Oftentimes you can start this process at the Ministry of Planning and Investment.	The official fees are nominal; the "adjusted fees" are not. Check the laws, and then check your pocketbook for a balance suitable to pay the officers' "expediting" fees.	14 – 21 days
2	Get your seal-making license. Without a company seal, you can't do much in Vietnam. Start this process at the Administrative Department for Social Order (ADSO).	VND20,000 (about $1.14)	About 1 week

Step	Action	Estimated cost to complete action	Estimated time to complete action
3	Get company seal made. There's a list of approved vendors at the Administrative Department for Social Order and you'll need to produce your original seal-making application and license to the seal maker.	VND200,000 – 400,000	About 1 week
4	Now that you have the seal, you can open a bank account. Shop around for a bank, as each has different minimum balance requirements and fee structures.	No charge	4 hours, if you have all of your paperwork organized in advance (resolution of the management board on authorized signatures, company seal, bank-issued application form).
5	Visit the tax department in order to apply for your business tax identification number and to pay business license tax.	The cost of the business license tax varies based on the amount of registered capital of your company.	About 1.5 weeks
6	Announce your new company in a daily newspaper – must include pertinent details such as: company name, address of HQ, branches or rep.	Costs vary depending on the newspaper chosen, size of announcement, etc.	About 1 week

Step	Action	Estimated cost to complete action	Estimated time to complete action
	offices, line(s) of business charter capital for limited liability companies, full name, home address, nationality, passport number, and the number of establishments of the company owner(s).		
7	Buy VAT invoices from the tax department or print your own self-printed VAT invoices.	VAT invoices can be purchased for VND16,000 for a book of 50 invoices.	About 2 weeks
8	Register with the Ministry of Labor, Invalids and Social Affairs (MoLISA) office to declare use of labor.	No registration fee	This step needs to be completed within 30 days of starting operations in Vietnam and should take less than 1 day to complete.
9	Register employees with the Social Insurance Fund for payment of health and social insurance for all employees with contracts of three months or longer.	No registration fee	Less than one day

CHAPTER 3
Establishing Your Presence

When you have made the decision to engage in a project in Vietnam or to pursue a business plan, you need to ask and get answers to several important questions: What legal framework will facilitate your business goals in Vietnam? Where should you base yourself: Hanoi, Ho Chi Minh City or one of the smaller towns and cities? Should you partner with a local company or try to go it alone? How do you find space for your office?

You might also wonder whether the size of your business venture is an important consideration. As with many issues in Vietnam, opinions differ. While the Vietnamese government likes large investment projects coming into the country and devotes more government resources toward companies that are investing on a grand scale, some business managers believe that it is easier for small companies to go through the licensing process. Big or small, it is important to use your resources appropriately and seek local assistance in navigating through the different government agencies, departments and ministries.

Starting out on the right foot is important. Try to learn all about (and take measures to avoid) the pitfalls that most foreign entrepreneurs have encountered. The less time and money you spend on problems, the more resources you'll have for establishing and building a successful business venture. The first reason most companies fail is cash flow, and the second reason, of particular importance in Vietnam, is how they set themselves up in the beginning.

GETTING STARTED: A VIETNAMESE PERSPECTIVE

Yahoo! Vietnam officially entered the Vietnamese market in August of 2007 through a Representative Office License; it began to enhance its legal presence and exploit its business prospects in early 2008. We met with Mr. Vu Minh Tri, the General Manager and Chief Representative of the Vietnam office. He was formerly the General Manager of Sony Ericsson in Vietnam and unlike most of the expatriates and foreign businessmen that have been interviewed for this book, Tri was born, raised and educated in Vietnam. He also studied abroad in Thailand and Europe for some of his business and technical training. His perspective is unique because he is an insider who knows the country, speaks the language and lives the culture. What he says is both enlightening and is contrary to many foreign business leaders' perceptions of business in Vietnam.

Tri believes the biggest mistake that foreign companies and businessmen make, before they even come to Vietnam, is failing to do an appropriate amount of research. Whether discussing market, legal or cultural problems with Tri, the theme of a failure to prepare permeates the interview and his perception of foreigners. Entrepreneurs assume that Vietnam will be close enough to what they have seen elsewhere, and that their experience will be relevant. While it is true that Vietnam shares the cultural attributes of many of its neighboring Asian countries, Vietnam has had a very unique and intense history riddled with conflict and social upheaval, much of which took place very recently. This history has contributed to the business environment, legal landscape and current culture.

Tri describes why Yahoo! decided to come to Vietnam, and it is obvious that the company did its market research. Tri lists a number of statistics that rank the country as among some of the world's most attractive for the internet service provider. With a gross population of 85 million there is an "internet population" of over 20 million. This 15-17 percent penetration rate is considered high. The growth in the penetration rate is also high and expected to reach 35 percent in the next few years. Yahoo! also found a high degree of commitment from the government in terms of infrastructure growth and willingness to engage the company.

The demographic of the country fits well with Yahoo's target customer profile. The country is considered very young with a majority of the population being the kind of youthful, trendy and forward-thinking individual that the company targets. Yahoo! is aggressively moving into mobile advertising, and Vietnam's high cell phone penetration rate (as discussed elsewhere in this book), coincides with the company's expansion plans.

Tri believes that foreign managers are unprepared for the country's regulatory structure. While he admits that laws and requirements are unclear, he believes that it is important to understand the rationale of the current structures. Tri states, "Foreigners are lazy in trying to understand 'why.'" Getting to the "why" allows for better understanding of the regulatory climate and a more flexible and adaptable attitude toward the legal requirements. Much of the business coming into Vietnam is new and unfamiliar to the government, but they do want to understand it. The government is very willing to help companies and makes efforts to smooth the process of working in the country, but the officials need to understand the new businesses, and the benefits for their country. Business is viewed as a relationship, and when the benefits to both parties are clearly outlined, it is possible to harness a spirit of cooperation from the government.

Tri also refutes the commonly held contention of many other business managers in Vietnam; that Vietnam is mostly interested in big money projects and businesses, and that dealing with the government and doing business in the country is much easier for big multinationals. He states that the government isn't just interested in bringing money into the country. This is too simplistic a view. In reality they have a far broader range of interests that in many cases a small company can satisfy. He contends that the government is willing to engage small companies, but he cautions against coming into Vietnam with a nervous and defensive posture, perhaps expecting corruption issues and challenges in dealing with the government.

Business leaders read about issues like corruption in Vietnam, from outside the country, and fail to engage the government appropriately. Resources come into play here as well, and small companies will direct theirs elsewhere. Small companies with limited resources often don't give high priority to protocol and government relations. Bigger companies can afford to address a broader range of important areas. Tri also argues that it takes big companies much longer to get licensed, as they typically need to get more permits and other licenses and are scrutinized more carefully. As noted earlier, the government needs to see the "mutual benefit" in a new company coming into Vietnam. It's a relationship. This is very different from the way business is viewed in the West.

Some useful advice also comes from Tri in regards to navigating the early licensing and permitting stages for a company. He suggests using a business consulting company in tandem with a law firm. Law firms understand the law and can act on your behalf in satisfying certain requirements. Many companies choose this route because they are fearful of doing this directly themselves and/or simply don't have the time and resources. A business consulting company will work with you to facilitate your engagement and communication with the government. This turns out to be more productive and speeds the entire licensing and permitting processes. This approach makes it easier for the government to understand what you want to do in Vietnam. Using both a law firm and a business consulting company will broaden the range of perspective a company develops in the licensing process, which can be gray and murky.

Finally, Tri states his views on corruption, which again run contrary to the mainstream views as espoused by Western business leaders and media reports. He says the system is similar to what is found in Western countries like the U.S. and Europe, but it is less clear and poorly organized. There are many structures in place to help you speed up licensing and adminis-trative procedures. The difference is that it is difficult to figure out how these structures work in Vietnam. Tri states, "In Vietnam, you go directly to the source. You pay the person who is assisting you directly. There are fewer middlemen [read lawyers and consultants] involved. You don't pay for a 'yes' or 'no' on a license or permit issue; you pay to speed the process and for services rendered."

Although Vietnam is more vague and opaque in its protocol, procedures, laws, and regulations, it is incorrect to view the process as corruption.

Foreigners are at a disadvantage to local Vietnamese in understanding the system, and they should hire professional help. The system will work the same way for both foreigners and locals alike. The difference is that foreigners pay more because they require consultants and legal assistance; the local Vietnamese won't.

LEGAL STRUCTURE

Deciding how to structure your legal presence in Vietnam is critical. There are five main classes of foreign investment in Vietnam. These include:

- 100 percent foreign-owned enterprise;
- joint venture;
- business cooperative contract;
- build-operate-transfer project;
- foreign investment shareholding company or joint stock company (FISC).

There are also different ways of structuring an investment in Vietnam under each of these main classes. As a 100 percent foreign-owned enterprise a company may choose to open a representative office, a branch of an existing foreign-owned enterprise, or a new legal entity altogether. Business cooperative contracts are used mostly in sectors where participation is restricted, such as mining, oil and gas, telecommunications and tourism.

As mentioned previously, the business structure that must be used and the percentage of ownership allowed varies by industry, and WTO commitment. The joint venture, business cooperative contract and build-operate-transfer project require a local partner interest or involvement in the business. These business structures also allow you to legally generate revenues within the country.

A Representative Office License (under the 100 percent foreign-owned enterprise class) gives you a legal presence in the country, but restricts your business activities. You cannot generate revenue within the country. The license is also not as easy to get as it once was, but is still a very common vehicle for initial entry. The Vietnamese government issued new regulations on this and Branch Office Licenses on July 25, 2006, under Government Decree No. 72/2006/ND-DP. Get used to seeing these "decrees" issued regularly. The legal landscape is constantly changing and many times the changes are made retroactive.

This new decree requires that a foreign company must have been in operation for at least one year from the date it was incorporated in the home country. This could prove particularly problematic for companies from Hong Kong and China, which only have validity periods of one year on their business registration certificates. Representative and Branch Office Licenses are no longer perpetual either. They are renewable but now limited to five years. Businesses that were licensed under this structure prior to this decree are given six months to complete applications for new licenses.[1]

The most important limitation of the Representative Office License is that the company is restricted from directly generating revenues in Vietnam. Companies use this license to get an understanding of the market before committing, to do market research, or to manage vendors and contractors who are operating in the country and exporting to their customers. For example, Nike has a Representative Office License and is heavily involved in the factories that manufacture its shoes. However, it does not own the factories and has no direct retail presence.

As mentioned previously, many joint ventures and partnerships fail. In Vietnam they fail for many of the same reasons that they fail elsewhere, but they also fail due to the ownership percentages. Vietnam was at war for much of the 20th century. The Japanese, Chinese, French and Americans all played a role in the turmoil that has plagued the country, and the Vietnamese themselves acted as invaders in Cambodia. This history makes the Vietnamese apprehensive about dealing with foreigners, and when a foreign enterprise comes in and pushes hard for a controlling interest (51 percent or better) of the business that is being established with a local partner, feelings of distrust and animosity can develop. This may not seem serious in the beginning, but an unequal share distribution can temper a feeling of inequality in general, and cause problems later in the relationship.

WORK PERMITS

Shortly after a company obtains a license, it must get work permits for any foreign staff who will be working in Vietnam. The permit process can be extremely arduous, so it's important to know what should be done before coming to the country and what can be done after you are there. It can be frustrating to realize that you don't have a document needed for the process, and the resulting delays can be costly. We spoke with Kim Holz, the program director for Embers Asia, a training company based in Ho Chi Minh City. Holz went through this process in late 2008, and the mechanics are still quite fresh in her mind. She notes that the most frustrating part of the whole process was how confusing it was to go to several different government departments just to get an accurate picture of what needed to be done. Holz says, "One of the most important things I've learned about work permits is to have a very good Vietnamese administrative assistant who understands this process and can assist."

To help us illustrate the Vietnamese permitting system, Holz provided the following outline of the process as well as the list of qualified exemptions. If you are saying to yourself "Oh my god" at the end of reading the following outline, then brace yourself. If you are laughing after reading it; perfect, you have the ideal personality for doing business in Vietnam.

Work Permit Exemptions

According to the Decree No. 34/2008/ND-CP dated March 25, 2008, any foreigner working in Vietnam must have a work permit, except in the following cases (Article 9):

- A foreigner entering Vietnam to work for a period of less than three (3) months.
- A foreigner who is a member of a limited liability company with two or more members.
- A foreigner who is the owner of a one-member limited liability company.

- A foreigner who is a member of the board of management of a shareholding company.
- A foreigner entering Vietnam to offer services.
- A foreigner entering Vietnam to work to resolve an emergency situation such as a breakdown or a technically or technologically complex situation arising and affecting, or with the risk of affecting, production [and/or] business and which Vietnamese experts or foreign experts currently in Vietnam are unable to deal with, [but] if for above three months then after working for three months in Vietnam the foreigner must carry out procedures to register for issuance of a work permit in accordance with this Decree.
- A foreign lawyer to whom the Ministry of Justice has issued a certificate to practice law in Vietnam in accordance with the law.

Outline for Process of Obtaining a Work Permit

I. Before submitting the application for work permit to the Department of Labor, the Company must announce its recruitment in a daily newspaper with three (3) consecutive articles.

II. Documents provided by the Company:
   a. Application for Recruitment of Expatriate,
      i. Signed and sealed by Company's legal representative;
   b. Notarized Copy of the Company's License;
   c. Application for granting work permit,
      i. Signed and sealed by the Company's legal representative.

III. Documents provided by the Expatriate:
   a. Application for working;
   b. Copies of Professional Certificates/Diplomas of Expatriate,
      i. Signature and seal of the Certificate's signatory must be certified by a public notary of the foreign country and legalized by the Embassy/Consulate of Vietnam in the foreign country;
      ii. Then translated into Vietnamese by the notary office of Vietnam or Company's legal representative.

c. Certificate of Noncondemnation:
   i. One (1) document from Vietnam police in Expatriate's residential area/ward stating you have no criminal records or violations during the time you have lived in the area.
   ii. If Expatriate resided in Vietnam over six (6) months, the Certificate of Noncondemnation must be issued by both Foreign authority and Vietnamese authority. (Two (2) certificates are required.)
   iii. One (1) document from local police department of last place of residence in Expatriate's country.
   iv. Signature and seal of the Certificate's signatory must be certified by a public notary of the foreign country and legalized by the Embassy/Consulate of Vietnam in the foreign country.
   v. Then translated into Vietnamese by the notary office of Vietnam or Company's legal representative.
d. Certificate of Health:
   i. Issued by foreign hospitals or issued by some specific Vietnam hospitals;
   ii. Approved hospitals: Cho Ray Hospital, Thong Nhat, Vietnam-France Hospital in Phu My Hung, Columbia, Oscat/AEA.
e. Curriculum Vitae signed by Expatriate.
f. Four (4) photos (3x4) of Expatriate.
g. Notarized (in Vietnam) copy of Passport.

Kim Holz also had some valuable comments on some of these different steps. In regards to the documents that need to be provided by the expat, Kim notes, "This is the most difficult step especially if you are trying to do this while in Vietnam. I am still dealing with trying to get this processed. It is definitely a lot easier to do if you are back in the States and a few of my friends actually went back to do all this. The law firm we are using even stated they have difficulties trying to get work permits, particularly for American citizens. The Certificate of Noncondemnation was handled for me by my landlord in Vietnam. I gave her my passport and she was able to initiate and handle the whole process. It was pretty easy to get processed quickly and I didn't have to worry about fees or waiting a long time at the police office."

For the document that needs to be provided by the police department from the expat's most recent foreign residence, Kim says, "This step is also easier to do while in the U.S. because they require fingerprints to process the criminal record. You can go to the U.S. Consulate here, do the fingerprinting and send it back to the police department of last residence or forward to a friend or family member who can 1) take it to the police department for processing, 2) pick up the completed criminal record for you, and then 3) mail it back to you in Vietnam."

In regards to the Certificate of Health that must be obtained, Kim comments, "This is the easiest part of getting the work permit. I don't recommend people going to the Vietnamese hospitals. Vietnam-France Hospital was really easy to do and the process can be finished in three hours."

RENTING OFFICE SPACE

Finding space for your office is fairly straightforward in the big cities. There are several well-established property agents in both Ho Chi Minh City and Hanoi, and there are English language newspapers that have classified listings of office space for rent. However, there is an acute shortage of real estate in general and specifically of Grade A office space. This has caused a rapid escalation in prices over the past couple of years with rates hitting $42 per square meter in Ho Chi Minh City and $45 per square meter in Hanoi in August 2007.[2] By October of 2008, these rates had climbed to a range of between $45 and $67 for Grade A space and between $25 and $45 for Grade B space, which included service charges but excluded VAT. Service charges cover cleaning and other necessary building maintenance. With the recent global economic downturn, the real estate market has shown definite signs of reversing these trends. Tenants have become more discerning as of late and the majority of office users are seeking rent at or below $45 per square meter.[3]

Massive real estate developments outside of the congested city centers are another option for companies that don't need to be in the heart of the city. Saigon South is a "new city" development that incorporates housing, office space, and important infrastructure amenities such as international schools, a hospital, restaurants and other shops. This development area is about 20 to 30 minutes from the Ho Chi Minh City central business district. Hanoi has several new areas, including Ciputra, which offers all of the amenities of the city. These options offer lower office rents in more modern and often better-equipped office buildings.

It is harder to find rental space outside the big cities, especially in the more remote areas. There are usually no office buildings, so your options are limited to shop houses, villas or private homes that can be converted into office space. In the very small towns you have to walk the streets and look for signs showing that a place is for rent, or ask around and rely on word of mouth to find your space. You can't pick up a local newspaper and search through the classified advertisements. It doesn't work this way outside of the big cities. While you will need to haggle over the rent, in general rates will be much lower than in the big cities.

The advantages to a lower rent can easily be overcome by the shortfall in basic services that are needed to run any business. One very important disadvantage of locating a business in a small town versus a larger city is the lower quality infrastructure. This can impact a business in a number of ways. Phone and internet services in small towns can be very poor; the system can become overwhelmed and connections slow to a crawl; and there are more black-out periods where there is no service. At a minimum this can be an inconvenience. Other infrastructure problems can include poor quality roads and unreliable power and water. The major infrastructure projects that are underway in Vietnam are mostly focused in the big cities, so the problems in remote areas are not expected to change soon.

In general, Vietnam rental contracts are the same as you would expect in more industrialized countries, but there are a couple of peculiarities worth noting. Maintenance fees and other necessities like internet hookup may be included in your lease. Landlords in Vietnam like to have large up-front payments for several months' rent. The typical contract will ask for six months payment in advance and sometimes even more. The 10 percent VAT is often not included in the rental rate negotiated and adds heavily to the overall payment. These unfavorable terms are a result of the current shortages in available office space and can be expected to dissipate as the supply of space increases and/or the current economic environment continues to cool. Negotiation is just as common in real estate as it is in the local vegetable and fruit markets. Patience and good humor will earn you more concessions than a hard-line attitude, regardless of the business climate.

EXIT STRATEGY

Every good business plan for Vietnam must include a well-articulated exit strategy, especially if sizable assets are moving into the country. In Vietnam, liquidating a business can be more difficult and expensive than setting one up. As a well-heeled businessman working in Vietnam for several years said, "If they don't get you coming in, then they'll get you going out."

We interviewed Luzius Wipf, a Swiss coffee baron who has been doing business around the world for almost two decades. Wipf came to Vietnam in 1998 and set up Asia Coffee Company Ltd. in Lam Dong province, about 300 kilometers north-west of Ho Chi Minh City in the south central highlands. Wipf was impressed by the amount of coffee grown in Vietnam and set up a factory to process and roast coffee beans. Later, he established coffee shops in Ho Chi Minh City and Hanoi.

In Vietnam, when you close a business, you need to secure stamped letters from all of the interested government entities, proving that you have honored all of your liabilities and commitments. The tax department, customs, and police are a few of the agencies you may have to visit, depending on the industry and line of business. After running his business successfully for many years, Wipf decided to liquidate and sell the assets to a Taiwanese tea farmer. The following interview illustrates the difficulties of closing a business in Vietnam:

BV: So Luzi, which was the first government department that you had to clear in this whole process?

W: I was visited by the customs department because I export coffee, and they wanted to audit my records from the past 10 years. I was surprised by this as they had never conducted an audit in the past.

BV: How long did the audit take?

W: Well, they came to my factory, and it took me and two administrative assistants a week to answer questions and provide the documents that they wanted. They questioned records going all the way back to the beginning and told me that I had not paid the correct duty on certain shipments.

BV: How did you settle up?

W: About a week ago, I found out that they had actually gone directly into my company account and debited the funds themselves [$4,000]. They didn't need any signed letter from me. They just went in and took the money they said I owed. I wasn't even offered a chance to contest this.

BV: Who did you have to deal with next?

W: The tax department came in as well and did a full audit on my books back to the beginning. They were supposed to have done an audit in 2004, but they never showed up. They contested everything from a telephone bill back in 1998 that they said was not allowed [could not be expensed], to all of the employee travel that we had taken as expenses. They wanted $14,000 in taxes.

BV: So what did you do?

W: I wrote a letter to the People's Committee and said that this was not fair. They should have come in and run the audit in 2004 like they said they were going to, and then I could have changed some of my accounting.

BV: And they decided in whose favor?
W: The tax department's. Fortunately, the labor department did not fine me for anything, and now I am finalized. My operations are finished. I am clear to liquidate my business and cancel my license if I want to.
(Author's note: It didn't cost Wipf anything to get his license ten years ago, but he did pay for it on the way out of the country.)

Embers, a training and consulting company based in Ho Chi Minh City, had a similar experience when it was restructuring and closing out one of its licenses in 2007. The company was operating under a Representative Office License, which restricts operations to market research and a couple of other non-revenue generating activities. When the legal representative for this company went into the service of trade and tourism, he learned that the company was required to issue a balance sheet report, which hadn't been filed for each of the five years it had been in existence. Of course, the representative questioned why a balance sheet report would be required for a company that only had a Representative Office License. No reason was given and as in the West, ignorance of the law is not an acceptable excuse. The end result was a $2,000 fine. The licensing fees were $60 from when he first opened his office and $1,500 in "consulting" fees to facilitate the license processing.

SUMMARY

Vietnam is not an easy market to enter or exit. The decision to do business here should be made with a full understanding of all of the differences and barriers in the Vietnamese business world. The structure of the business and the location need to be considered very carefully, with an insight into factors that are important in Vietnam, such as infrastructure, which is a "given" in a developed country. It also takes time and resources to discontinue operations, which can add insult to injury if the business was ill-conceived from the beginning. A good business plan should include a comprehensive study of the market, a solid plan for entry and a good understanding of what the process will entail if the company decides to conclude its business activities.

ENDNOTES

1. Official Gazette of Vietnam, July 30, 2006.
2. "Vietnam's Real Estate Market is Booming," *AsiaOne Investor Relations*, July 19, 2007, http://www.asiaone.com/Investor%2BRelations/Industry%2BNews/Story/A1Story20070719-18890.html
3. "The Hanoi Real Estate Market Q3/2008 Update and Special Feature: New Housing Options—East & West," CB Richard Ellis, October 23, 2008.

CHAPTER 4
Navigating the Business Landscape

Coming into Vietnam and being able to function effectively is essential to the success of any expatriate business manager. This is particularly challenging due to the recent emergence and "newness" of private business in the country. For a very long time, and until only a decade ago, there was no such thing as private business. Success was not rewarded. There was no business culture and no such thing as "profit." These are all new concepts and ideas that are being introduced into the country. One of the biggest mistakes an expatriate manager can make is to assume that the business climate in Vietnam will be anything like what they are familiar with.

Business managers used to be considered the top of the food chain and beholden to no one (except the government). They were perceived as superiors who sat around all day drinking coffee and smoking cigarettes. Employees did what they were told, and no one questioned authority. People aspired to hold management positions in the government because legally the government was the only employer in the country.

But with private business being allowed to develop and thrive by actually making money, this stereotype of the "manager" has been largely broken down. The multinationals have come in and introduced the "Western business manager." Big improvements have been made; however, almost everyone you will be dealing with grew up in a different system than the current one. Stopping previous habits and practices is far more difficult than learning something new, in the same way that it's harder to tear a building down and rebuild it, than it is to start from scratch. But this is what needs to be done. As much emphasis needs to be placed on the unlearning as on the learning.

Some of the vestiges of the old system are still around and present themselves as formidable barriers. While you might be able to change some practices, there are others with which you will have to conform. The way a foreigner navigates the business landscape in Vietnam will determine whether he achieves some level of success or leaves the country disgruntled, jaded and pessimistic about the entire experience.

BUSINESS PROTOCOL

Meetings

Vietnam is just as hierarchical as other Asian cultures, but maybe not as formal. The country is generally Confucian in philosophy, and respect and deference should always be made to those in authority. Handshakes are the form of greeting and the more senior members of a meeting should be introduced first. Women often shake with two hands, but you should wait until a woman extends her hand first and if she doesn't, a slight bow of your head is appropriate. Meetings are arranged the same way as they are in the West and punctuality is expected. Meetings with businessmen and with any government agency are very difficult to arrange a week before, the week of and a week after *Tet* (Vietnamese New Year). This is particularly true with government organizations, and important documentation that needs to be pushed through a government agency should be scheduled around this time. *Tet* follows the lunar calendar and is the same as the Chinese New Year.

The exchange of business cards and business card etiquette is the same in Vietnam as it is in much of Asia. It's a good idea to have one side of a business card translated into Vietnamese, while the other side can be in English. Business cards are given and received with two hands and are looked at carefully by both parties. It is more respectful to leave the business cards of all those attending a meeting out on the table in front of you; don't put them in a shirt pocket or wallet until the meeting is concluded.

Business Attire

Business dress in both Ho Chi Minh City and Hanoi is relatively formal and conservative. Long sleeve button down shirts are worn and depending on the industry, ties may be appropriate. Women wear business suits and skirts that go below the knee. Most office buildings are air conditioned, so the heat and humidity only get uncomfortable when you leave a building. Dressing too informally may be construed as a sign of disrespect among the older and more conservative segment of the population.

Business Entertaining

When entertaining a business client, the expectation is that the person who has issued the invitation will pay for the meal. There are two toasts that you should be familiar with: The first is *tram phan tram* (100 percent) which indicates that you should drain your glass in one gulp. The other is *chuc suc khoe* which translates as "good health." Again, it is good form, but not imperative, to drain your glass. The Vietnamese love their karaoke and it is probably the most common pastime after a business dinner. This is a chance for business associates to see each other in a less formal setting. Usually a business dinner will conclude fairly quickly. People also don't tend to stay out very late and an evening's activity would typically conclude by 10:00 pm.

Time Sensitivity

In general, there is much less sensitivity to time in the business climate here. The further you get outside of the big cities, including Ho Chi Minh City and Hanoi, the more you will find that punctuality is less of a priority than it is in the West. Consensus-building, relationships, social structure and etiquette are more important to the Vietnamese than timeliness. An employee would think little of showing up to work late because of a personal problem at home.

Consensus will always be sought, even if it means not making a deadline. A future appointment will be sacrificed in order to tactfully and respectfully end a current engagement. A common understanding that people are doing the best they can under the circumstances is assumed, which works fine until you throw another culture's time sensitivity into the mix.

CORRUPTION

Unfortunately, an envelope with money in it is still how business is expedited in Vietnam. There is a very thin line between the "red envelope," which is traditionally used at New Years and other holidays in Asia to give "gifts" to family, friends, employees and business partners, and the envelope passed to a government official to help speed your license approval. At first you will be shocked at how deep this practice goes. To be successful in Vietnam, you will need to expect it and effectively deal with it. Applying Western ethics to the situation will create difficulties, but blindly giving in to the practice may compromise one's own personal integrity. A thoughtful approach to where the line should be drawn is warranted.

As published by Transparency International, the Corruption Perceptions Index shows that Vietnam ranked 123 of 179 in 2007; in 2008 it ranked 121 of 180. Lower numbers show a higher level of perceived corruption, while higher numbers show less. Countries like Denmark and Singapore show the lowest levels of corruption, while countries like Myanmar and Zimbabwe are perceived to be the most corrupt. Expert assessments and opinion surveys are used to create the table. The survey generally targets the size and frequency of bribes in the public and political sectors to create the ranking. Table 4.1 shows that in 2008 Vietnam was ranked with Nigeria, Sao Tome and Principe and Togo, which gives an indication of what to expect when dealing with public officials.

At its most basic level, corruption probably hurts the common citizen in Vietnam the worst. The traffic police are notorious for being particularly ruthless in enforcing the law. When people are tempted into breaking a law,

Table 4.1   Corruption Perceptions Index

Country Rank	Country	2008 CPI Score	Surveys Used	Confidence Range
121	Nigeria	2.7	7	2.3 – 3
121	Sao Tome and Principe	2.7	3	2.1 – 3.1
121	Togo	2.7	6	1.9 – 3.7
121	Vietnam	2.7	9	2.4 – 3.1
126	Eritrea	2.6	5	1.7 – 3.6
126	Ethiopia	2.6	7	2.2 – 2.9
126	Guyana	2.6	4	2.4 – 2.7

Source: Transparency International

whether it's speeding, carrying goods on top of a vehicle, or carrying too many people on one motorbike they find themselves in a compromising situation with the police. Of course, the risk is calculated as most people know exactly what it will cost to avoid a ticket.

Corruption in Vietnam is not limited to just the public sector. It permeates the economy and is deeply entrenched in the private sector as well. As mentioned in the "Local Competition" section of Chapter 9, there is quite a bit of "under the table" money, which finds its way into the competitive bid processes in Vietnam. As also mentioned, participation by American companies in this type of activity is in violation of the Foreign Corrupt Practices Act, and other countries have laws against this practice as well. Companies found engaging in this practice face stiff penalties from both their home countries, as well as the government of Vietnam. This is not the only way that corruption manifests itself in private business. It also finds its way into everyday business in a way that can add significantly to a company's cost structure.

With so much shady business going on, it is no surprise that local staff have begun to adopt the practices that have been set before them as example. One manager of a small training company in Ho Chi Minh City describes the problem he has encountered:

"We have to send staff out to buy materials for the training events that our company conducts. Most of the items are small-priced and can be purchased readily around town at a number of different locations. I didn't pay much attention to the costs until I noticed that they were going up. This continued for some time before I decided to go to the market to try and find some of the items that were purchased. I was surprised to find that they were much cheaper than the receipts the staff was showing for them. I questioned the staff about this and got long-winded explanations about how there were many places to buy these items and they were buying from a trusted friend. So we decided to require that all items be purchased from just a couple of main stores in town. We also started to require that legal 'red' tax invoices (the only invoices accepted by the Vietnam taxing authority for expenses) were obtained on ALL purchases. This would surely stop the problem. I was suspicious that staff was pocketing the difference between what an item actually cost, and what they were claiming. I thought these legal tax invoices should resolve the issue.

It didn't. On one particular event that was very last minute, I had to go into one of our supplier stores and pick up about $100 worth of presentation materials. At the counter I explained that I worked for XYZ Company and that I needed a red invoice. 'No problem' was the response I got and a red invoice was presented to me for $110. I was told that for the red invoice I would need to pay an extra $5. Apparently the retail staff at the store and my staff were each making 5 percent on every transaction conducted there!"

A brief comparison with taxing procedures in the United States and Europe is necessary to fully understand this situation. In the West, when a company spends money, it keeps a copy of the receipt and claims the expense against its revenue. The receipt can be hand written, or be simply the cash register receipt from the transaction. In Vietnam this is not allowed. For an expense to qualify as "legitimate" a government-issued red invoice or a government-approved company invoice must be provided. These invoices have all of the company details from both sides of the transaction

Red invoices are a huge source of corruption in Vietnam. For a while there were companies that would set up shop just to sell tax invoices. Companies would buy them to increase their costs and reduce their profits, thus decreasing their tax liability. The fraudulent shops would quickly go out of business and shut down before their racket could be uncovered. The amounts on the tax invoices these companies were selling could be in amounts greater than $10,000. The government has mostly put a stop to this by better regulating the registration procedures for local companies and by going after every company that purchased a tax invoice from these fraudulent businessmen.

Why is there all this fuss about red tax invoices? To start with, taxes are relatively high in Vietnam, and a company that issues a tax invoice must pay value added tax (VAT). This is also how the government tracks a company's revenue, and corporate profit taxes are based on how many tax invoices are issued and their total value. There is a strong disincentive to issue a tax invoice. At the same time companies desperately want to receive tax invoices on purchases they make because only these expenses can be claimed as "official." There is a vicious cycle where every company wants to receive tax invoices but nobody wants to issue them. The corruption that is propagated by this system includes tax evasion (by the companies), theft (by the employees), and fraud (by the entities issuing incorrect invoices). The blame of course should not fall exclusively on the system itself. It is a trickledown effect to the general population from its mentors in government and business.

Moonlighting in the Western world means working a separate job for additional pay after your normal work hours, but it takes on a whole new meaning in Vietnam. Partially out of desperation, people look for a "side business" to supplement the low incomes they receive and generate additional income in creative ways from the jobs for which they're already being paid. For example, many employees will base their decision to use a certain supplier or go with a certain vendor based on what's in it for them personally.

In the public sector, the government is aware of this problem and is making a concentrated effort to address corruption on multiple fronts. Two of the main target areas are 1) streamlining the processes for government approvals and permits and 2) improving the pay and education of government employees.[1] By streamlining the administrative processes there should be more transparency and less ambiguity, which should result in less opportunity to take advantage of the system. By improving pay, there should be less incentive to engage in corrupt activities, and educational improvements could be a long-term solution to the corruption problem. The hope is that by setting an example at the government level, the ethics will filter down to the business community, and a more ethical business environment and level playing field can be created.

The media is also doing its part to eliminate corruption by reporting incidents (It Is regularly reported on in the mainstream media). A high profile case involving the Transportation Ministry was covered in two of Vietnam's largest daily newspapers in 2005. In 2006 the Transportation Minister was forced to resign and several other officials were arrested. The scandal involved millions of dollars in foreign aid money being gambled away on football matches.

The reporting is not completely free, however. Journalists need to be careful about what they write. Two Vietnamese journalists were brought to trial in May of 2008 for their reporting on this case. Reporters Nguyen Van Hai and Nguyen Viet Chien are known for their aggressive reporting on corruption, which has resulted in them being charged with "abusing freedom and democracy." They could each receive seven-year jail terms.[2]

NEGOTIATING WITH THE VIETNAMESE

"Face" is the most important Asian concept to understand in order to successfully negotiate in Vietnam. Just as in other Asian countries, a culturally sensitive approach needs to be used to successfully get what you want. Causing someone to lose face almost guarantees that the negotiation will fail. Face concerns the trust, confidence and respect that a person's social standing and position confer upon him. It's important not to embarrass a person or make him look bad in the eyes of his co-workers and subordinates. A loss of face can be brought about overtly by intentionally making someone look inferior or wrong. It can also be brought about subtly, through slight embarrassments. "Polite" lies should be accepted and all efforts should be made to keep dignity intact.

It is expected that there will be at least some element of negotiation factored into every facet of business in Vietnam from the local market to the boardroom. This can be very frustrating for the average foreign manager who will most likely be familiar with a far more open system of doing business, where goods and services are more clearly priced. As in much of Asia, patience is the key to successful negotiation with the Vietnamese. Items for sale don't have price tags in the local markets, although in the bigger city marts and grocery stores they do. In the market, the more patient a person is, and the longer he is willing to engage the seller with a smile on his face, the better price he will get. The more impatient and rushed a person is, the worse the price he will get. Negotiation is a game to the Vietnamese, and it is a game that they enjoy. Be a good sport and take the time to engage them, and you get rewarded. Become agitated and appear rushed and you pay the price.

The bartering attitude and culture of constant negotiation have been brought into the workplace as well. Labor contracts, although signed and finalized, will not serve to keep a local staff member from requesting a large increase in pay or other benefits not outlined in his/her contract. It's important to make sure that staff is clear, not just on the terms of their employment, but also on how long it will be before the terms are re-evaluated. Employee reviews are important. Consistency is important as well. If an exception is made to a rule, then that rule becomes null and void and difficult to enforce in the future. Unfortunately, this limits an employer's ability to do "extra" things to reward employees. The extras become expected and might as well be written into future contracts. Management actions have a way of setting precedents.

The challenge of constant re-negotiation of terms, on everything from labor contracts to partnership agreements and project bids, has been exacerbated by the recent high rates of inflation in the country. The inflation rate in 2007 was already at 7.3 percent, but by August of 2008 it climbed to almost 30 percent year-on-year.[3] With such a radical shift in prices, it has become difficult for employees to maintain their standard of living. Many can't wait for the once yearly reviews and adjustments in salary. Large construction projects find themselves in huge cost over-runs because of the rise in building materials costs. Potential partners see their overall returns evaporated by the same forces.

The problem of contracted terms not being viewed as final cannot be blamed solely on inflation. The business climate is very Asian in this respect; the value and importance of relationships outweigh contracts and other legal documents in terms of importance. When circumstances change, pre-negotiated terms are fair game for re-negotiation. It's important to understand this. Even when inflation abates in Vietnam, this cultural and business attribute will still remain. Putting the value of a long-term relationship first will protect and buffer any existing and future agreements.

Vietnam's business practices will probably evolve towards more Western practices. There will be more protection for foreign parties that enter into agreements in Vietnam, but the value of patience and flexibility in the negotiating process will remain important.

DEALING WITH THE DIFFERENT GOVERNMENT DEPARTMENTS

Customs may be the most frustrating of all the government departments. The rules seem to change at whim, and if you don't have a connection with the customs authority, you could run into some expensive roadblocks. The following example illustrates the types of problems you may encounter.

Biking trips are extremely popular in Vietnam because until recently much of the populace used bikes as their primary mode of transportation. Many of the world's top tour operators offer some kind of biking experience in

Vietnam with the most popular being the North to South ride which puts you on part of the old Ho Chi Minh Trail that was used during the Vietnam War. Many ground operators started businesses to cater to this market segment, and to avoid requiring clients to bring their own bikes, they all try to bring in high quality bikes.

The tariffs on the importation of bikes clearly state that bikes that are imported for resale are subject to 20 percent duty. Bikes that are imported for operations, or company use within the country, are subject to a much lower duty or none at all. The problem that none of the companies foresaw was that customs expect you to prove that the bikes are not being brought in for resale. It is impossible to prove you aren't planning to sell them. How do you get your bikes that are sitting at the port collecting storage released? By paying the 20 percent duty, or you may be able to find assistance through one of the customs officials (which isn't free of course). Alternatively, you could have a letter from the People's Committee that basically tells the customs officials to back off. You obviously need a key contact in the People's Committee for this.

Several of the leading adventure travel companies in Vietnam have encountered this issue including Exotissimo Travel, Handspan Adventure Travel, Phat Tire Ventures and even the ultra high-end Butterfield and Robinson (B&R). B&R was importing a particularly large shipment of more than 70 bikes into the country from Canada in 2005 when they ran into their problem. They had to re-export the bikes from Vietnam and bring them in under a different mechanism. The whole exercise was most likely very frustrating and certainly expensive. The only way to prevent this problem is to ensure that when a company is being licensed the imports that it needs for operations are explicitly stated in and covered by the license.

Customs don't cut importers any slack on documentation. The slightest inconsistency or omission on a document will put an importer at the mercy of the customs officials. The penalties are stiff, and the people you get to deal with are typically not very customer service-oriented.

One way to deal with the inevitable trips to the different ministries, service and tax departments is to have a local staff member allocated to the task.

Alternatively, most of the law firms offer services that include everything from helping to obtain a work permit to the full range of pre- and post-licensing and registration procedures. Law firms can get expensive and are not necessary for most administrative procedures. There are certain instances when a foreign manager will need to go into a government office, and, at a minimum, a local staff member should be brought along for translation purposes. The local government offices appreciate this gesture as it makes dealing with foreigners easier. Many of the government staff members don't speak English very well, and although they will accommodate any foreigner who comes into their offices, it clearly makes them uncomfortable.

You won't be given a courtesy call by the People's Committee if something important changes that has an impact on your business. Keep abreast of business policy and procedure information by reading regular legal update newsletters, such as Allens Arthur Robinson Vietnam Legal Update newsletter. This can be subscribed to for free at http://www.aar.com.au/general/subscribe.htm.

The various chambers of commerce are also good sources for specific legal updates, and many have newsletters that are published frequently. The U.S. Consulate does a weekly newsletter on Vietnam-U.S. trade and investment, http://www.amchamvietnam.com.

Another government agency to be aware of, particularly if you're going to be doing business in one of the outlying provinces on the coast or near the border with Cambodia, is the Border Police. There are still certain areas in Vietnam that are off limits to foreigners, even though there are no signs saying so in Vietnamese or English. These areas are typically in very remote villages along the coast or near the land borders with other countries. Foreigners have been held and questioned for hours and even overnight. Vietnam is very sensitive to its territorial integrity, and this, coupled with old-fashioned attitudes the further away you get from the big cities, can cause problems for foreigners.

One expatriate told us about an experience he had going into a remote fishing village that he was considering bringing his staff to for a retreat. He and his guide were pulled into a military compound right on the beach and questioned for over three hours. The police simply could not comprehend what a foreigner would be doing out in the remote countryside of Vietnam.

IMPORT AND EXPORT CONSIDERATIONS

Bringing goods into (and exporting product out of) Vietnam can be administratively challenging. There is a degree of vagueness in the regulations and the customs authority often interprets the tariffs in ways that are detrimental to a company. As cited in the earlier bike tours example, the burden of proof in determining whether or not your product meets the requirements to qualify for a preferential tariff rate is borne by the company. The company that brought bikes into Vietnam for operational purposes ended up paying a substantially higher tariff rate (20 percent versus 5 percent) because it could not prove that the bikes were not for resale.

As mentioned earlier, the solution to import challenges is to obtain the necessary import permits and to detail the imports that you plan to bring in for your business in the licensing phase. This requires foresight and forecasting everything that might be needed up to several years out. Detailing your company's import requirements and the duty rate that you will be subject to in your license can help you avoid unfavorable interpretations of the commercial code by customs personnel.

BANKING AND MONEY MATTERS

The Vietnamese currency is the dong. As of this writing, the current exchange rate of the Vietnamese dong (VND) to the U.S. dollar (USD) is about 17,800 to 1. Over the past seven years the exchange rate has steadily moved upward with the VND depreciating from about 15,200 to its current rate.

In the past few years, Vietnam has changed its currency from paper notes to the polymer or plastic type notes that are seen in other countries. They have also started issuing coins for the first time in many years in 1,000, 2,000, and 5,000 denominations. The most common denomination notes of the new paper currency are 10,000; 20,000; 50,000; 100,000 and 500,000.

Banking

After receiving its license, the first thing a company does is set up a bank account. There are a number of reputable foreign banks in Vietnam including

HSBC, Citibank, Deutsche Bank, ANZ Bank and a host of more regional banks. All of the documentation that is created in the licensing and registration of a business needs to be brought in to set up an account, including the license itself, tax code and company stamp paperwork and appointment letters. The police department issues the company stamp paperwork when the official company chop (stamp) is granted, shortly after licensing.

Companies typically set up three accounts; the capital account, a VND-denominated account and a USD-denominated account. A capital and VND-denominated account are required. A USD account is not required, and an account can actually be set up at one of the big multinational banks in almost any major currency. The capital account is used to bring in the legal capital that a company has committed to investing into the country. This is the investment of the company in its business in Vietnam. The legal capital of a company is clearly outlined in its license and the amount of this legal capital must be transferred into the capital account, typically within a period of between six months and two years. The capital account cannot be used for payments or other banking activities. Funds must be transferred into the company's other accounts before it can be used for those purposes.

Banking in Vietnam is not as easy as it is elsewhere. Overseas payments to vendors need to be supported by documentation including invoices, contracts and bills of lading if products are being paid for. Likewise, transfers within the country should be supported by government-approved invoices from the vendor if the expense is to be allowed by the government for tax purposes. Unsupported transfers are typically refused by the tax authority thus increasing a company's VAT and corporate taxes. Great care should be taken in this area.

Repatriating Profits

Profits can be repatriated out of Vietnam. There is actually no tax on dividends paid to shareholders. The only condition is that the legal capital requirements that a company has been licensed under need to be fulfilled. When a company is licensed in Vietnam, it commits to investing a certain amount of capital in the business it is starting. The government likes this amount to be high. Companies prefer that the amount be small, because it is a binding commitment. It is something that needs to be negotiated in the licensing phase of a business set up in Vietnam. This is the capital requirement. The company's corporate taxes must also be paid. Of course, documentation must be provided to the bank in order to process the transfer, and as this seems to change with each bank, it is best to check well before attempting the transaction.

Exchange Rate

Vietnam maintains a managed floating exchange rate regime. The State Bank of Vietnam sets the official exchange rate, and the currency is allowed to move within a trading band on either side of the established rate. When the exchange rate becomes more volatile, the government often restricts the trading band to within 1 percent, and when there is less volatility, the trading band is relaxed.

This system works for the most part, unless there is a major disruption or strong economic current working against it. In September of 2008, coinciding with the financial crisis being felt in the United States and elsewhere in the world, the Vietnamese dong exchange rate became very volatile. The government lost control when a black market emerged offering substantially higher rates for currencies such as the U.S. dollar than was being offered by the banks. The black market only lasted for a couple of weeks and then disappeared.

The dong is not easily traded outside of Vietnam. Thus, the currency is not viable for international transactions and not accepted as a medium of payment by international vendors.

Figure 4.1 shows the depreciation of the Vietnamese dong from January of 2002 through the end of 2008 in both U.S. dollar terms and Japanese yen terms. A steady decline in the value of the Vietnamese dong can be seen with a more erratic period of fluctuation coinciding with the world financial crisis in late 2007 and 2008.

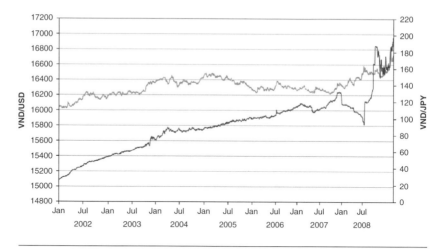

Figure 4.1 Depreciation of the Vietnamese dong
Source: Bloomberg

Interest Rates

Interest rates in Vietnam fluctuated wildly during 2008 due to the emergence of very high rates of inflation. On June 10, the State Bank of Vietnam raised the prime interest rate to 14 percent from 12 percent in an attempt to curb inflation. Deposit and lending rates were also correspondingly increased from 14 percent (deposit) and 18 percent (lending) to a maximum of 21 percent for lending.

This was the third time the bank had increased interest rates since February 1. Before February, interest rates had remained unchanged for three years.[4] At first glance these interest rates may seem attractive. But inflation in the country is actually higher than the rate paid on deposits, and the country has gone through periods of extreme currency depreciation that would make the returns negative when converted into another currency. For example, if you put VND1,000 in the bank and received an interest rate of 15 percent, but inflation was 20 percent, then you would actually be losing 5 percent of your purchasing power in Vietnam over the period of one year.

The same could be said for the impact of the exchange rate on your return. If you changed U.S. dollars into Vietnamese dong and put the money in the bank at 15 percent interest, and the currency depreciated by 20 percent then you would be losing 5 percent of your money in U.S.-dollar terms.

Pricing and Naming Considerations

If a company is going to be selling within the country, and its target customers happen to be foreigners, as might be the case in tourism, an important matter to consider is how your prices are denominated. The law states that prices must first be in Vietnamese dong and then can be listed in another currency, which can pose problems given the fluctuating nature of the currency. Fortunately, it doesn't seem like many companies comply with this regulation, and the government doesn't seem to enforce it. In fact, in Ho Chi Minh City, in almost any of the trendy shops in District 1, almost all of the prices are listed in USD, and if they aren't listed, then they are quoted in USD when a sales person is queried. The government can, of course, decide to selectively enforce the law.

The sign that marks a company's place of business is also regulated. If a company has a Vietnamese name and English name, the Vietnamese name is supposed to be listed first, and in bigger letters than the English name. This peculiar law seems to get enforced more rigorously in the outlying and remote provinces. The way around the law is to only register an English name when licensing the company. It's important to be careful with this one, especially if the company is going to have branch offices outside of Ho Chi Minh City, Hanoi or the other big cities. Company signs must be submitted to the responsible ministry for approval prior to public display.

The logo of a company has to be registered before it can be put on a company's sign. Companies have had their requests for approval of signs refused because of the lack of documentation supporting the logo. The government does not do a great deal to support the intellectual property of a company, including its logo and trademark, even when it is properly registered. Evidence of this can be seen in both Ho Chi Minh City and Hanoi, where there are copycat restaurants and tour agencies right next to the more successful and established businesses, sharing the same name, logo and menu of meals or tour options.

SUMMARY

The business landscape in Vietnam is unique. And it is evolving, which complicates it further. However, many of the cultural characteristics of the business environment are remaining unchanged, and an understanding of these can prove extremely valuable. The more dynamic issues such as corruption, a wildly fluctuating currency, the ever-changing rules and regulations and dealing with different government agencies require patience. A calm approach best serves the foreign manager. It's important to not let the ambiguities of the business environment sour you on business in Vietnam. After all, everyone is dealing with the same challenges and what proves difficult for you has most likely proven difficult for everyone else as well.

ENDNOTES

1. *Vietnam Business Law Handbook*, 2008 4th Edition, Global Investment Center, Washington D.C., page 28.
2. "Vietnamese Journalists On Trial for Stories," October 14, 2008, cnn.com/asia, http://edition.cnn.com/2008/WORLD/asiapcf/10/13/vietnam.journalists.ap/index.html
3. "Background Note: Vietnam," U.S. Department of State, Bureau of East Asian and Pacific Affairs, August 2008, http://www.state.gov/r/pa/ei/bgn/4130.htm
4. "Vietnam Raises Prime Interest Rate," June 10, 2008, *China View* (www.chinaview.cn), http://news.xinhuanet.com/english/2008-06/10/content_8341131.htm

CHAPTER 5

The Labor of Labor

OVERVIEW OF THE LABOR LANDSCAPE

Developing economies tend to implement rigid and cumbersome labor rules that are meant to protect their workers from exploitation. Rules can make it difficult to hire employees, to ask employees to work flexible hours, and to reduce the size of your staff. Vietnam is considered to be a fairly rigid human resources environment in which to operate, as compared to best practice locations such as Singapore and the United States, where the governments allow more labor market flexibility.[1]

Here's a look at what to expect from the labor market, as well as some of the statutory and common human resources practices in Vietnam.

WHAT TO EXPECT: LOCAL CANDIDATES

With the influx of foreign investment come high expectations from the local labor pool. There's a hierarchy of desirability when it comes to employers: if you are a well-known global company, you'll be in high demand with local job seekers, next comes less well-known but still international companies, followed by regional companies, and then finishing with local Vietnamese companies. The reason to work for the foreign companies is clear: most foreign companies pay higher than the local firms, and offer more advancement or educational opportunities.

From the online job indicator of Table 5.1, you can assume that there are three qualified applicants for every four jobs available. Five percent

Table 5.1   Online job supply and demand indicator

	Q1/2007	Q2/2007	Q3/2007	Q4/2007	Q1/2008	Q2/2008
Labor Supply	8,864	11,580	10,719	10,794	15,101	15,101
Labor Demand	10,550	15,025	15,964	17,647	20,647	20,712

Source: VietnamWorks

unemployment, as Table 5.2 shows for 2007, is often considered merely a transactional figure, meaning that everyone who wants a job has one; and some workers are in transition between jobs. The high demand for talent, coupled with the lack of experienced applicants leads to a very tight labor market. However, as Vietnam's inflation and economic concerns increase, the labor market seems to be on the brink of a cooling down period. Some sources believe that the cooling had already begun in the second half of 2008.

The pool of working-age local Vietnamese talent is a relatively large and young population. Forty million Vietnamese are of working age, of which about half are under 35. Ten million of these candidates live in urban areas. Every year, about one and a half million new workers enter the labor market, of which more than half a million are university graduates with abundant job opportunities before them. Thus, finding interns and entry-level staff isn't a problem. However, while it has been quoted that 30 percent of the urban

Table 5.2   Vietnam's unemployment rate

Date	Unemployment Rate (est.)	Percentage Change
1995	25.00 %	
2003	6.10 %	−75.60
2004	1.90 %	−68.85
2005	2.40 %	26.32
2006	2.00 %	−16.67
2007	5.10 %	155.00

Source: CIA *World Factbook*

population is proficient in English, some managers say that finding candidates with truly proficient English language skills is their biggest challenge. Twenty-one percent of the local workforce is described as technically skilled, but some managers say there is a need to clearly define the skills needed in modernized work environments. For example, many job applicants for positions in offices will unfortunately not be proficient users of Microsoft Office applications.

Finding and keeping upper echelon staff is a top priority for foreign firms operating in Vietnam. There aren't enough experienced middle managers or senior-level leaders available, as compared to the abundance of recent college graduates. Because of Vietnam's unusual war-induced demographic profile, there is a scarcity of trained, well-developed talent available. With over 50 percent of the population under the age of 35, the talent gap is quite pronounced in the middle and at the top of the job pyramid. The Vietnamese are intelligent and are intrinsically capable of performing their functions, but as a result of the country's history, the people lost contact with global best practices and lacked access to quality, relevant education, especially in the areas of soft skills and people management. While the country focused on rebuilding and rehabilitating itself, critical years were lost for employees who needed modern business experiences in preparation for middle management and senior-level roles. Many candidates lack an appropriate level of business knowledge for working effectively with (and competing with) their international counterparts.

One trend that worries employers is that the most capable employees often leave their employer once they've gained critical skills and try to establish their own businesses. Vietnam is becoming a land of entrepreneurs, and copy-cat businesses abound.

Another concern for companies in Vietnam is the job opportunities that each well-trained and capable employee has available; many companies in Vietnam promote prematurely just to keep their people on-board. A common profile of a middle or senior-level Vietnamese manager is someone who is over-educated, under-experienced, over-confident and under-committed to their organization, which results in a massive number of unrestrained job-hoppers.

SUMMARY

Developing countries offer opportunities for developing everything, including people. Be sure to have reasonable expectations when recruiting for your local workforce, especially around specific job experience, Western-style management know-how, and English language skills. Your employee retention strategy must include a substantial training budget for improving the skills that you need most. You must also ensure that you're developing talent for middle-management and senior-level positions.

SKILL SET GAPS

A September 2008 interview with Aidan Lynam, the CEO of Holcim Cement Vietnam Ltd., revealed some interesting insights into Holcim's experience in coming into the Vietnamese market. Holcim Cement was an early entrant into the Vietnamese market, establishing their presence in 1995. Aidan was one of the pioneers tasked with the human resource initiative of getting a local staff ready to run the $350 million dollar investment the company was making. The goal was to have the "human assets" trained and ready to work at the same time as the factory and other equipment became operational.

Aidan notes that one of the most shocking (and enlightening) experiences he has had in the 12 years he has worked in the country, happened when Holcim officially opened for business in 1997. After two years of training, the select staff of Holcim employees was ready to start work at the new plant. "There was a complete and total inability to transfer the knowledge learned in the training over the previous two years to the practicalities and reality of the workplace," Aidan states. "I completely overestimated their ability to deal with the work challenges we had trained them for." Aidan says that the staff had an incredible desire and ability to learn and a very strong work ethic. However, the soft skills like creative problem solving, effective communication, and leadership had not been trained alongside of the hard-skill, technical knowledge. The employees had not been taught how to apply the technical skills they had learned in situations calling for leadership and human interaction. The local managers had not been taught how to lead, problem-solve or communicate effectively in the new setting they were placed in. They were unsure about their role and appropriate actions when faced with a real management dilemma.

This was a costly mistake for Holcim, and it's one that many companies make. The staff had been carefully selected and was off the charts on all of the technical hiring criteria. They were "red hot" according to Aidan, but the project implementation progress slowed as execution issues surfaced, including intervention in problems, providing direction for frontline staff, and implementing the management systems which had been built and taught in the pre-operational phase. Aidan had to bring in a skeleton team of foreign expatriates to help run the business at considerable expense and loss of time.

What does Aidan say he would do differently if given the chance for a "do over"? "Train the soft skills equally or even more than the hard technical skills. The Vietnamese can learn the technicalities. It's the soft skills that need to be emphasized. You need to send them overseas very early in the pre-operational phase to see how actual business processes operate, how the human factors need to be handled, and to witness firsthand the real-life, daily challenges that occur. Expose key players to practical projects for a year before they have to lead in Vietnam. That's what I would do differently."

So how do you go about recruiting Vietnamese talent? What do the Vietnamese look for in an employer and what attracts the best talent? How do you select the best candidate to run your office for success in the Vietnamese business environment?

To ensure the best possible candidates for your Vietnamese operation, Winnie Lam of Navajos Group advises several recruitment and retention strategies:

- Recruit constantly. If you wait until you have an opening, you will be too late.
- Use your staff as talent scouts. In Vietnam, employee referral programs are not only good recruiting tools, but also they help with retention.

- Leverage your brand for recruiting and retention; people want to work for companies with "brand name" products.
- Engage in service projects for the good of the community. Corporate social responsibility is one of the key factors Vietnamese expect from an employer-of-choice.
- Use internships and management trainee programs to recruit and develop supervisory staff.

WHAT TO EXPECT: THE *VIET KIEU* CANDIDATE

Viet Kieu translates roughly as "overseas Vietnamese," and is used as a label for any ethnic Vietnamese that reside outside of Vietnam, especially those that have been outside of Vietnam for many years.

A major multinational manufacturer thought that they had struck gold when they found Mr. Nguyen. This highly educated Vietnamese had been living in the U.S. for several years and was willing to return to Vietnam to assist with the company's Vietnamese operations. He was given a full expatriate package, even though he carried a Vietnamese passport, given the number of years he had spent outside of his mother country. As part of this package, he was assigned a car and a local Vietnamese driver for his and his family's use. Unfortunately for the company, they didn't know that this particular overseas Vietnamese candidate had a very serious flaw; he regarded the Vietnamese as second-class citizens. He was reputedly very rude and insensitive to his driver. For example, he refused to let his driver off duty to attend the funeral of a close family member. Mr. Nguyen's behavior so infuriated his driver that he, along with several other drivers from the company, beat him up. Mr. Nguyen had to be sent out of Vietnam for his own protection from future assaults. He was later fired from the company.[2]

In a team-building exercise for a mixed group of finance professionals, the participants were asked to take turns saying what they needed to see more of from their teammates, by starting their request with "What I need from you is. . ." When one of the participants turned to a Vietnamese man, he addressed his *Viet Kieu* colleague and said, "What I need from you is for you to be more Vietnamese." To which his *Viet Kieu* colleague replied, "That will be difficult for me, as I have lived most of my life in Texas!"

Returning ethnic Vietnamese are increasingly being courted by foreign companies doing business in Vietnam. They are often considered a bridge between the foreign entity and the local market. Many are returning to rediscover their cultural roots, to care for extended family, or to live well in a country where domestic help is readily available and the cost of living is much lower than most developed locations.

Reasons for choosing a returning Vietnamese national instead of a non-Vietnamese expatriate usually include: accelerating the pace of entering Vietnamese markets, mitigating the talent shortages in the local labor market, better alignment with local customs and practices, and training local staff more easily in the native language. The compensation package for *Viet Kieu* talent is in line with their market demand. However, this is not always a less expensive option as compared to employing a foreign national that is not ethnically Vietnamese.

Unfortunately, many returning Vietnamese face unique challenges, as compared to expatriates of other nationalities. Some claim that they have greater difficulty being accepted by their local peers, others have trouble applying their overseas experience in their "home" market, and their international levels of pay as compared to their local counterparts can cause conflict in the organization.

There are stories of *Viet Kieu* employees treating the local staff very harshly, and also stories of the local staff alienating *Viet Kieu* employees.

These issues may stem from the fact that many of the *Viet Kieu* were affiliated with the Southern Vietnamese during the war, or it may simply be jealousy stemming from the *Viet Kieu's* oftentimes larger paycheck and relatively more affluent lifestyle. In addition, if the *Viet Kieu* employee has a foreign-born spouse and children, the spouse and children may consider the quality of life in Vietnam to be much lower than they had in their "home" country (that is, medical care, parks and cultural issues).

WHAT TO EXPECT: WORKING REGULATIONS

Chad Ovel, the former managing director of ScanCom Vietnam Ltd., provided some stern warnings on making sure that the labor laws are fully understood. ScanCom, a 100 percent foreign-owned Danish furniture manufacturer and retailer, was one of the three largest exporters from Vietnam in 2004 and 2005 and had realized explosive growth during Mr. Ovel's six-year tenure. The company was exporting close to 900 containers of furniture a month and was second only to IKEA and Nike in terms of overall export value out of Vietnam.

Mr. Ovel describes an interesting situation that took place at one of the company's warehouses outside of Ho Chi Minh City in 2005. Most warehouses in Vietnam require a security check of staff leaving the premises because of the high degree of theft that takes place. On one occasion, a cleaning lady was caught with toilet paper and other cleaning supplies in her backpack. The security guard detained her and she was immediately fired from her job. There was a security tape of the incident to verify the security guard's testimony. The worker, when faced with the filmed evidence, signed a report admitting to the attempted theft.

The cleaning lady, however, then filed a case against ScanCom for wrongful termination. Ovel decided to fight it in court on principle. ScanCom lost the case and was forced to pay the cleaning lady an entire year's back wages and to allow her to have her job back. The company had made a couple of mistakes. Apparently this was not the first incident involving this particular employee, but the company had not documented the previous incidents. You are allowed to terminate an employee for theft, with or without a prior offense but ScanCom had made a second mistake: They never invited the police into the warehouse to formalize the termination of the employee.

Three months after the employee was allowed back to work she was terminated again. This time there was proper documentation, and the police were notified. The labor laws are designed to heavily favor the employees in Vietnam. Any mistake in procedures will be used against a company, regardless of the nature of the employee's infraction. Knowing the labor laws is not enough. Knowing the correct processes that need to be followed in conjunction with these laws is also essential.

WAGES

According to a report by the Ministry of Planning and Investment, the average wage of a laborer in the foreign direct investment sector is around $75–$80 per month; the average salary of an engineer is about $220–$250; and that of an administrative officer is close to $500.

The average wage for all Vietnamese in Vietnam is approximately VND824,000 per month, or roughly $55.[3] While the figure is not a precise measurement of wages, it does confirm that labor is cheaper in Vietnam than in most other countries.

Wages in foreign companies are often higher than in domestic ones operating in the same sectors, and wages in foreign-local joint ventures fall somewhere in the middle.

There are considerable geographic differences in remuneration levels within Vietnam. The average monthly wage in Ho Chi Minh City is approximately VND1.5 million per month, while in Hanoi and Quang Ninh, a smaller and less-developed city by comparison, it is about 1.2 million. Besides the geographic differences, and differences between foreign-invested companies and local companies, certain industries pay higher than others. At the high end are companies operating in advertising and media, as well as companies that offer financial services. At the low end are manufacturing and property development/construction firms. And in terms of function within the company, you can expect to pay more to your marketing, finance and accounting teams as compared to your administrative services and operations teams.

According to Navigos Group's Vietnam Salary Survey Report for 2008, annual salary increases reached 19.8 percent—the highest increment within the last five years. This was a dramatic increase, given that the economy was booming in 2006 and 2007 and the salary increases in those years were recorded at only 12 percent and 12.6 percent respectively. Table 5.3 combines statistics from the Navigos survey and the Asian Development Bank to illustrate salary increases and inflation from 2004–2008.

Interestingly, the highest average wage increases were not being granted by foreign-owned companies. The highest increases were going to employees of local Vietnamese companies, as the local companies struggle to close the gap between their lower wages, and those offered by the multinationals operating in Vietnam. Local Vietnamese companies averaged 20.2 percent wage increases.

The results of this survey also revealed that some companies are conducting salary reviews two to three times within a year, with the percentage of increase and frequency in varying degrees. This is primarily in response to the inflation issues facing employees and retention issues facing companies operating in Vietnam.[4]

Most companies will divide annual wages by 13, in order to deliver one month's salary as a *Tet* bonus. While performance bonuses are still relatively new to the market, they do work as an excellent retention tool. Giving out the bonus in smaller, more frequent payouts is one technique to keep the local staff with your company.

Table 5.3   Average base salary pay increases and inflation, 2004–2008

Year	2004	2005	2006	2007	2008
Wage Increases	8.0 percent	9.5 percent	12.3 percent	12 percent	19.5 percent
Inflation	7.9 percent	8.4 percent	9.0 percent	12.6 percent	27 percent (est.)

Sources: Navigos Group, Asian Development Bank

Another retention and reward technique is to offer an employee savings plan, where the company matches the employee's savings at a certain percentage with a vesting schedule set over a time period, such as five years. An employee savings plan, although new to the Vietnamese labor market at this time, has proven to be an excellent retention tool for companies that offer it.

WORKING HOURS

Vietnamese law provides for an eight-hour working day or a 48-hour working week. The employee may work overtime, but the overtime should not exceed four hours per day and 200 hours per year. In certain special cases stipulated by the government, overtime hours can be increased to a maximum of 300 hours per year.

Businesses in all economic sectors, including businesses with foreign-invested capital, are encouraged to adopt a 40-hour working week.

Workers who are under 18 years old and women who are over seven months pregnant or with a child of less than one year in age are granted an extra hour off a day and are not permitted to work overtime.

There is a minimum requirement that a 30-minute rest break be given for every eight-hour workday, or 45 minutes for working a night shift. Although work hours vary from business to business, they tend to fall between 8:30 am and 5:30 pm, with a one-hour break for lunch between 12 noon and 1:00 pm for office positions.

There must be 12 hours between shifts, and employees need one full day off for every week's work or average of four days off in a month. In addition, the company must provide an additional 30 minutes off in every working day with full pay for any female employee in her menstruation period.

OVERTIME

Employees may work up to a maximum of four hours of overtime a day and 200 hours (or 300 hours in some special cases) a year. Employers must compensate workers according to overtime pay rates. Overtime during normal working days is paid at 150 percent of the normal rate, whereas employees working night shift overtime must be paid at a minimum of 180 percent of their usual hourly rate of pay.

Employees working during weekends and on holidays without taking other days off are entitled to earn 200 percent or 300 percent respectively of the normal rate.

ANNUAL LEAVE

An employee with one year of service is entitled to an annual leave with full pay. The annual leave will be classified as follows:

- 12 days for a person working under normal conditions;
- 14 days for a person involved with heavy, noxious or dangerous job activity or working in places with harsh living conditions or for persons under 18 years of age; and
- 16 days for persons involved with especially heavy, noxious and dangerous job activities or working in places with especially harsh living conditions.

The number of days of annual leave is increased proportionally to the period of employment in an enterprise or with an employer by one additional day for every five years of employment.

OTHER LEAVE

Remember, Vietnam is a socialist country, and companies from countries with more employer-friendly laws, or from countries with more stringent and limited leave policies, must be prepared for the differences in the Vietnamese business world. In addition to the paid statutory public holidays, as illustrated in Table 5.4, other leave includes:

Table 5.4   Statutory public holidays with pay

Holiday	Date	Number of Days Off
Solar New Year	Jan 01	1 day
Lunar New Year	per Lunar calendar	4 days
Death Anniversary of Hung King	Mar 10	1 day
Victory Day	Apr 30	1 day
International Labor Day	May 01	1 day
National Day	Sept 02	1 day
	Total Number of Holiday Days	9 days

Sick Leave

- Up to 40 days annually with less than 15 years of social insurance contributions;
- Up to 70 days annually with more than 15 years of social insurance contributions;
- 75 percent paid through Social Insurance Fund with proper documentation;
- 25 percent paid by employer (voluntary).

Child Care Leave

- 20 days a year if the child is less than three years old;
- 15 days a year if the child is three to seven years old;
- Only one parent is entitled to the above;
- But the other parent will be entitled if child is still sick after the stipulated days.

In addition, up to 65 percent salary is paid for up to 180 days to take care of a sick child.

Maternity Leave and Special Benefits

- Up to six months with 100 percent salary paid through Social Insurance Fund with cap.
- Coverage is calculated per average of last six months prior to leave.
- Additional allowance worth two months of minimum wage.
- Must subscribe to social insurance for six out of last 12 months before delivery to qualify.
- Five physical examination days off with pay during pregnancy.
- Mother can return to work before finishing statutory maternity leave upon certification from doctor and will qualify for 100 percent pay from employer while collecting the social insurance benefits at the same time.
- Work must be reduced by one hour daily from 7th month of pregnancy until child is 12 months of age with full pay.
- Expectant mother and new mother must not be assigned overtime work, night work or work that requires significant travel.
- During the time of pregnancy, maternity leave, or nursing a child under 12 months of age, the female employee shall be temporarily exempt from unilateral termination.

Marriage and Death Leave

If there is one thing that we've learned about living in Vietnam, it is this: don't meddle with or try to shorten your employee's marriage and death leave. These are very, very important ceremonial days for most Vietnamese. Table 5.5 outlines the number of entitlement days for this leave.

Table 5.5 Marriage and death leave

Marriage and Death Leave	Number of days
Own marriage	3 days
Marriage of children	1 day
Death of parent, spouse's parent, spouse, son or daughter	3 days

WORKING AGE

The minimum working age in Vietnam is 15. An apprentice at a job training center must be at least 13 years of age, except in the case of certain jobs approved by the Ministry of Labor, War Invalids and Social Affairs. In any case, employees must be sufficiently healthy to satisfy the requirements of the job.

RECRUITING PROCEDURE

You may recruit Vietnamese employees directly or you can contract an employment service agency to recruit for you. When you hire an employee, you must notify the local authority in charge of the State Administration of Labor of the names of the candidates you have selected. Many Vietnamese job seekers are using online recruitment sites, such as VietnamWorks (www.vietnamworks.com), which is popular with many multinational corporations as well.

LABOR CONTRACTS

The labor contract must be in writing and in accordance with the model labor contract issued by the Ministry of Labor, War Invalids and Social Affairs. Verbal agreements may be entered into with domestic servants (i.e. maids, gardeners, etc.) or temporary workers working for less than three months. For contracts lasting less than three months, a written contract is not required. A labor contract can be one of the following types:

- An indefinite term labor contract is a contract in which the two parties do not determine the term and the time for termination of the validity of the contract.
- A labor contract for a specific or seasonal job with duration of less than 12 months.

- A definite term labor contract, which is a contract in which the two parties determine the term and the time for termination of the validity of the contract as a period from 12 to 36 months.

The probation period can last up to a maximum of 60 days for jobs that demand a special skill, but it is 30 days for other jobs. The salary of a worker during the probation period cannot be less than 70 percent of the agreed salary.

During the probation period, contracts can be terminated by either party without a notice period and without payment of insurance indemnities.[5]

In a country where the labor laws weigh heavily in favor of the employee, the choice of which contract to enter into is important.

The general manager of any enterprise with foreign investors must also sign a collective labor agreement with the workers no later than six months after commencement of operations. Along with other issues agreed to between management and the workers, this collective agreement must include items such as the salary for each type of occupation, working conditions, labor protection, collective welfare and social insurance. The agreement is valid for a minimum of one year and a maximum of three years.

By law, workers' contracts may be terminated in cases of failure to carry out their tasks, breach of discipline (for example, absence from work for five days a month or 20 days a year without valid reasons) or other misconduct, or serious injury or illness. Companies may also dismiss employees because of financial problems at the company or the addition of technology that makes workers' jobs obsolete.

The length of notice for termination is specified in the individual labor contract. The minimum notice length is 30 days for definite labor contracts, 45 days for indefinite labor contracts and three days for project-based or seasonal contracts. A dismissed worker may appeal to the local labor agency for reinstatement. A retrenchment (severance) allowance must be paid.[6]

Much care must be taken with any retrenchment exercise in Vietnam; consult an experienced labor lawyer before taking action. While the laws do state that employees can be dismissed for a number of reasons, in actuality it is very difficult to terminate employees even when they are not performing their assigned duties satisfactorily. In addition, if the courts deem that an employer unlawfully terminated an employee, stiff penalties often apply. The employee must be re-employed and must be paid compensation equal to the amount of lost wages. If the employee refuses to return to work, the employee must be paid lost wages. Additionally, payment must be made equal to half a month's salary for each year of employment plus allowances, such as meals, transportation, and health care.

COMPULSORY INSURANCES

There are three compulsory insurances applicable to every employer and employee who has passed the three-month probation period (excluding expatriates). The first is health insurance. Both the employer and the employee must make health insurance contributions to the Social Insurance Fund. The employer pays 2 percent of the total wage fund and the employee is required to pay 1 percent of his/her salary provided in the labor contract.

The second required insurance is the social insurance. The monthly employer contributions are as follows:

- 15 percent of total salary fund from Jan. 2007 to Dec. 2009;
- 16 percent of total salary fund from Jan. 2010 to Dec. 2011;
- 17 percent of total salary fund from Jan. 2012 to Dec. 2013;
- 18 percent of total salary fund from Jan. 2014 onwards.

The monthly employee contributions are as follows:

- 5 percent of her/his salary from Jan. 2007 to Dec. 2009;
- 6 percent of her/his salary from Jan. 2010 to Dec. 2011;
- 7 percent of her/his salary from Jan. 2012 to Dec. 2013;
- 8 percent of her/his salary from Jan. 2014 onwards.

The third is unemployment insurance, which applies to (a) employees who are working in a company with an indefinite term or a term lasting between 12 and 36 months, and (b) employees who work for companies that have ten or more employees. Both the employee and employer contribute one percent of the employee's monthly salary to the unemployment insurance fund, as outlined in the labor contract.

EMPLOYMENT OF EXPATRIATES

Generally, the government of Vietnam discourages the employment of ex-patriates. If the foreigner commits to training a local replacement, he/she is seen as a positive addition to the local labor market. Unlike Singapore and other countries with "foreigner-friendly" policies, Vietnam has prohibitive rules about the number of foreign employees a company can hire. It also taxes expatriates' worldwide income, which makes it very complicated and expensive to use expatriate labor in Vietnam. The Labor Code stipulates that foreign-invested companies, branches and representative offices must give priority to the employment of Vietnamese labor. They are allowed to employ expatriates to work in Vietnam only if there are no qualified Vietnamese staff members or workers. Employers must plan and offer training programs to help the Vietnamese qualify for and replace the foreign nationals who are hired for skilled positions. The current labor law limits the number of ex-patriates employed by a company (including foreign-invested companies) to 3 percent of its total employees.

In order to work in Vietnam, foreigners must obtain a work permit from the Department of Labor, War Invalids and Social Affairs of the province/city where their employer is located prior to signing labor contracts with their employers.

Expatriates who are transferred within their enterprises to Vietnam can expect that 20 percent of the total number of managers, managing directors and experts are Vietnamese citizens.

However, a foreign-invested enterprise is allowed to employ at least three foreign managers, managing directors and experts.

Foreigners working for businesses, agencies, and organizations in Vietnam for three months or more must get work permits, except the following cases:

- Foreigners who are members of a limited liability company with two or more members;
- A foreigner who is the owner of a one-member limited liability company;
- A foreigner who is the member of a joint stock company's management board;
- Foreigners entering Vietnam to handle emergency cases, such as foreign lawyers who have been granted job practice permits by the Vietnamese Ministry of Justice as allowed by the law.

SUMMARY

In order to be successful in finding and keeping the right talent in Vietnam, your company will need to recruit constantly, offer a creative rewards strategy, and know the regulations governing employment in Vietnam.

Your employees will be grateful for training opportunities, especially if the training occurs overseas, and most young Vietnamese are excited to learn and to contribute to the organization. Establishing a pleasant work environment where the employee can see a track for upward mobility is also important in keeping your key staff onboard and engaged.

ENDNOTES

1. The World Bank Group and International Finance Corporation's Doing Business Project, www.doingbusiness.org
2. Names have been changed to protect the guilty.
3. Vietnam Household Living Standards Survey (VHLSS) 2004.

4. "Salary Increase Highest in the Recent 5 Years—Navigos Group Unveils its Preliminary Results from the Vietnam Salary Survey," Navigos Group Press Release, September 4, 2008, http://www.vietnamworks.com.vn/pdf_files/salary-increase-highest-in-the-recent-5-years.pdf

5. Labor regime explanation, Ho Chi Minh City Investment Trade and Promotion Center (ITPC), http://www.itpc.hochiminhcity.gov.vn/investors/how_to_invest/labor_regime/index_html/mldocument_view/?set_language=en

6. "Labor in Vietnam," Vietnam Trade Office in USA, http://www.vietnam-ustrade.org/index.php?f=news&do=detail&id=35&lang=english

CHAPTER 6

Working with Local Business Partners

When you decide to come to Vietnam for business purposes, it is very important to consider your entry strategy. In addition to the business license you decide to operate under, the choice of a partner is one of the first strategic moves you'll make. Even though Vietnam has recently joined the World Trade Organization (WTO), and the market must open many of the doors that were previously closed, most of the required changes will be phased in over many years.

Certain industries in Vietnam remain "restricted," and you must comply with certain requirements and special procedures. In this sense, Vietnam is very much like other parts of Asia that protect specific industries and require local partner ownership in the established business. The decision to find a partner may not be an option; it may be a requirement if your business is in the mining, telecom, and tourism sectors or other sensitive market segments.

Beyond the legal requirements that would require you to find a partner, there are other compelling reasons. If you lack experience doing business in Asia and more specifically in Vietnam, a local business partner can help you navigate the labyrinth of administrative requirements and connect with the different government organizations. A local is going to have market insights that no foreigner will ever have, no matter how long he's lived in Asia.

However, hiring a local partner also adds to the risk of your business venture failing. Countless businesses have collapsed in Vietnam due to a disagreement between partners. How do you protect your interests? You must understand that Vietnam's business environment is different from the West. For example, in Vietnam—and most of Asia—a contract is merely a guideline, the first step in a relationship, a flexible agreement that evolves over time. In the West, contracts in general are binding. In Vietnam, it is difficult to adequately protect your interests in a contract. The legal system heavily favors the local partners in business disputes. Therefore, leverage (using the power you have to its fullest) and protecting yourself need to be structured into your business plan.

WHY DO YOU NEED A PARTNER?

Vietnam was admitted into the WTO on January 11, 2007. This historic event meant that Vietnam is required to liberalize many of its markets and subject them to international competition, as well as open up many of its industries to foreign investment. Not everyone in Vietnam welcomes the upcoming changes, particularly some of the state-owned enterprises (SOEs). Nguyen Van Thoai, Deputy Manager of Saigon Cosmetics estimates that the perfume and toiletries retailer will see its market shrink by 20 percent after all of the WTO-mandated changes are implemented in his industry, and the market opens to new competition.[1]

What this means for those interested in entering the Vietnamese market is that the requirements and obligations that might compel them to seek out a local partner are slowly being removed. This doesn't mean that the need for a local partner has disappeared, but the reasons for linking up with a counterpart may become more business rather than regulation-driven.

It is not within the scope of this book to detail all of the WTO changes that are forthcoming, but a couple of important WTO-driven changes that have already occurred include the elimination, one year after accession, of the 30 percent foreign equity limitation for acquisition of Vietnamese enterprises. There are certain restrictions of course, but in essence this means that foreign businesses can now buy more than a 30 percent interest in Vietnamese companies. Many companies may choose this particular strategy as an entry strategy into the market and as a more equitable way to partner with Vietnamese businessmen.[2]

The phase-in period for different industries is also important. For engineering companies looking to capitalize on the massive infrastructure projects being launched in the country, for a period of two years from the date of WTO accession, 100 percent foreign-invested enterprises may only provide services to foreign-invested enterprises in Vietnam.[3] This means that a 100 percent foreign-invested engineering company would not be able to do any infrastructure work for the Vietnamese government. They would need to work through a local partner to secure the contract. These phase-in periods are different for different market segments and industries.

Many industries will remain very restricted even after all of Vietnam's WTO commitments have been phased in. Companies and individuals interested in doing business in the tourism sector will still be required to set up joint ventures. And foreign telecommunications companies will still not be allowed to provide network infrastructure services in Vietnam.

It makes very good business sense to have a local partner in certain industries in Vietnam. One of the primary challenges foreign managers face is navigating the country's bureaucracy. It is difficult to comply with the government's reporting requirements, and penalties accrue, which is a waste of time and resources.

If you are trying to sell into the Vietnamese market, you are going to be dealing with a completely different culture with unique tastes and preferences. Products that appeal to the average Westerner may be of little interest to the Vietnamese, and vice versa. Vietnam's history is unique, and history is what shapes a lot of what appeals to people. The status symbols in the West are your house and your car. In Vietnam they are your motorbike and your cell phone. The early movers into these markets have made huge profits as the Vietnamese have progressed from riding bicycles to riding Honda Dream motorbikes. What may make little sense to you is common sense to a local businessman.

Efficiency is the most compelling reason for pursuing a partnership as part of an entry strategy into Vietnam. You hire local accountants to do your accounting, marketing and sales professionals to generate business for you, and IT people to maintain your network. These people understand the work and the peculiarities of the market in relation to it. So partnering with a local that understands the business climate better than you do makes sense for the same reason. Vietnam is arguably much more complicated than many other markets one could choose to enter, so a "local expert" is very important. Partnering with someone who knows how things work can save your company both time and capital.

Many companies hire a "local expert" instead of pursuing a formal business partnership, and it works quite well if you are in an industry that is allowed to set up a 100 percent foreign-owned business. But hiring someone won't buy you the same level of commitment as developing a partnership with him, and in Vietnam commitment is crucial. Employee turnover is a huge problem here, unlike the loyalty found in Japan and other parts of Asia. People "job hop" regularly between the multinationals in Ho Chi Minh City and Hanoi, and because the labor market for talent in Vietnam is so tight, they get away with it. Gaining the serious commitment and genuine loyalty of your "local expert" extends well beyond the risk of having him leave for another company. In Vietnam, everyone is a businessman, and with intellectual property rights largely not enforced, your partner soon could become your competitor. If you own a small- or medium-sized company, with a less complicated business model, the incentive to copy what you do is high.

One example is Sinh Cafe, a local tourist transportation company who gained a dominant share of this quickly growing sector of the market in the late 1990s. It soon found itself surrounded by copycats, some of whom went so far as to completely copy the name and logo of the original. Copyright and trademark laws do exist in Vietnam, and you can legally protect your brand, but the onus is on the victim, not the offender, to identify the infringements and to push the authorities to enforce the laws.

Another good example is the case of Exotissimo Travel. This French-owned and -operated company has been extremely successful in the fast-growing tourism sector. They brand themselves high-end and are very accomplished marketers. The marketing director for Exotissimo, who was responsible for much of the content on the company's website, was surfing the web one day a couple of years ago when he came across a replica of the Exotissimo website. The only thing that had been changed was the logo, and it was only slightly changed. The color schemes, layout, and program contents were all identical. He was able to get the copycat website shut down, but it took time, effort and follow-up. Two weeks later another clone took its place.

FINDING A PARTNER

Vietnam did not legally recognize private business until 2000, so partnerships are a new concept in the private sector. All partnerships needed to be approved by the SOEs, or entities controlled and owned by the government. Many of the SOEs in Vietnam have been privatized. In the 1990s, there were about 12,000 SOEs, but according to Vu Tien Loc, Chairman of Vietnam's Chamber of Commerce and Industry, today only about 2,000 are still fully owned by the state. Vu Tien Loc projects that by 2010 there will be only 500 left, and these will be in highly sensitive areas such as defense and telecommunications.[4] The government is still heavily involved in business, however, and even though there is a massive push towards privatization, there is still a high degree of regulation of businesses.

Vinamilk, a dairy company based in Ho Chi Minh City, is the poster child for the government's plans to privatize state firms. Vinamilk is one of the fastest growing brands in the country and was also one of the first to extend its operations across all of Vietnam, from Ho Chi Minh City to Hanoi. The company has gone from a modest beginning of supplying its customers with sweetened condensed milk in tins after the war ended, to supplying premium fresh milk products in competition with multinationals, like global giant Dutch Lady.[5]

Many sectors of the economy are still dominated by entrenched SOEs, and although Vietnam is committed through the WTO to liberalize, the process is slow. Like China, Vietnam has come up with excuses as to why certain deadlines for freeing up segments of the market have not been met.

Aidan Lyman, the CEO of Holcim Cement Vietnam Ltd., discussed his experience with the company's joint venture partner, Hatien Cement #1. This state-owned cement manufacturer was also a major brand and so well recognized in Vietnam that people didn't order a bag of cement; they ordered a bag of Hatien. Cement manufacturing is categorized as a Class A industry, so Holcim was (and still is) required to have a local partner. Holcim also quarries much of the raw material that goes into their cement products, which is considered a mining activity.

The joint venture between Holcim Cement and Hatien #1 is a 65 percent (Holcim) – 35 percent (Hatien) split. There were more reasons than just legal requirements for partnering with a local company; the licensing and permitting that were needed to get started were much more easily facilitated by a local company. Permitting and licensing never seems to end in Vietnam, according to Aidan, so the administrative burden alone warrants a relationship. Today Holcim is in the process of increasing their investment in Vietnam by $650 million, and ironically their long-standing partner Hatien for the past 12 years is one of their primary competitors in the marketplace. Aidan states that their successful partnership is testament to the kind of flexibility and open-mindedness that is required for a successful business relationship in Vietnam.

PROTECTING YOURSELF

The Popcorn Jeff Story

Jeff was an American who came to Vietnam with big dreams of starting his own business and radically changing his career. He was formerly a police officer in Minnesota. Jeff had been to Vietnam before on a vacation and was captivated by the sights, smells, sounds and general bustle that were so different from back home. It was exciting and dynamic. Jeff saw opportunity all around him.

After visiting a local movie theater one day, he noticed that one very key ingredient was missing from the whole experience. Beside the fact that his ears were ringing from the maxed-out volume of the theater speakers, he realized that there was nothing to munch on while watching the film. Popcorn! he thought. Jeff was from the midwest, and the thought of bringing one of his favorite movie snacks to the Vietnamese theater experience was tempting.

As Jeff walked around Ho Chi Minh City and thought about his brilliant idea, he saw other opportunities for his product all around. In bars and restaurants there was little to salt the mouths of patrons and get them to buy more beer. Street vendors could sell popcorn as easily as any of the other snacks they were peddling. By the end of the week he was determined to pursue his business idea.

Jeff quickly learned that the laws are constantly being amended, and getting good information about business requirements almost always requires a lawyer. Businesses classified as retailing, which his would be, are heavily restricted from foreign participation. In order for Jeff to make his dream a reality, he would need a business partner—one who would actually be the sole owner of his business entity within the country.

"No problem," thought Jeff. "I'll find someone I can trust. Then I'll bring in the popcorn from the U.S. and he'll help me distribute it here. As long as I control the supplies, then even if I don't actually own the business in Vietnam, I will still have control over it."

Jeff did find a partner, and one that he thought he could trust. The business boomed and Jeff was proved right in his speculation that Vietnam needed popcorn. He built the business up to the point where he was importing five, 40-foot containers of popcorn seed every month, and he was branching out into selling popcorn machines to many of his bar and restaurant customers. Things were going great and he was making fantastic money. Of course, it was all through his partner as he was the one who actually held the license.

After doing business in Vietnam for a couple of years, a bombshell landed on Jeff's world. While he was in the office of his partner one day, Jeff came across a set of books that he hadn't seen before. In the books were three columns. One column was a list of numbers that Jeff was familiar with. These were the prices that the theaters, bars and restaurants paid for popcorn. In the second column was a list of numbers that were about 10 percent lower than those in the first column. A third column, titled "profit," showed the difference between the two. Jeff slumped into a chair as the reality of what had been happening over the past couple of years hit him.

This type of scenario plays out daily at different levels and in different ways at almost all companies in Vietnam, including the big multinationals that have exceptional controls and documented procedures. Skimming is an expected part of doing business in Vietnam; Vietnamese companies even budget for it, particularly restaurants.

This situation did work out in the end for Jeff, but he lost his business partner, a good percentage of his profits from two years of work, and he now has a competitor in the market. His partner was able to start importing popcorn seed on his own. What is the point of this story? Trust is important, but leverage through a control of some integral part of the business is crucial, particularly in restricted industries in which your business is dependent on a partnership.

Where did Jeff make a mistake? He didn't leverage the value that he brought to the partnership, and he didn't protect it properly. He probably should have structured his business more carefully and set up a company outside of Vietnam, which in turn would be the partner entity. The Vietnamese are eager to learn how the West does business, not for the sake of making foreign companies or individuals rich, but rather for their own benefit. Vietnam is still a poor country and its people feel enormous pressure to improve their position in life. You should expect that your business partner will put the long-term interests of himself and his family in front of your interests.

HOW TO APPROACH AND STRUCTURE A PARTNERSHIP

The Osborn study of 2003 showed a joint venture failure rate of 30–61 percent worldwide, and that 60 percent failed to start or faded away within five years.[6] Joint ventures in developing countries show greater instability and those with government partners have a higher incidence of failure than joint ventures in the West. Despite the risk, in Vietnam, a joint venture is sometimes the only legal mechanism for a foreign enterprise to do business in the country.

A large number of partnerships, whether they are structured as joint ventures, agent contracts, business cooperative contracts, or supplier agreements, fail in Vietnam. These failures can generally be blamed on a divergence in expectations between the foreign entity and the local one. What each party expects to get out of the relationship ends up being different from reality. The failures can be blamed more on the early stages of defining the business relationship and operational procedures, rather than how the business progresses after the agreements are finalized.

Most foreign enterprises place a great deal of confidence in and importance on the contract that they will be working under in Vietnam. More important than a legally binding written contract is the quality of the personal relationships that are built through daily conversations and actions. This is the real covenant by which the business relationship is governed. The conversations that are conducted every day, and what is said and done is far more important than what is written. Trust is the critical component, and trust is built up over time, not with the signature at the bottom of a contract. This is true not only in Vietnam, but also in much of Asia. This is not to say that the contract terms are not important; they are and every contract should be heavily scrutinized before a commitment is made. However, the contract becomes worthless if the personal relationship falls apart.

A much higher probability for success occurs as you prioritize the "relationship" over the "contractual agreement" in Vietnam. Also, you need to remember that there is much less of a distinction between what is considered personal and business. Explanations for why things are done are often given within the framework of a personal situation. With this in mind, the foundation and building blocks of the business relationship are the gifts that are exchanged, time for dinner and drinks and the interest shown for your partner's personal life and well-being. A business partner who becomes your friend secures the business relationship.

MANAGING YOUR BUSINESS FROM ABROAD

Because of the difficulties of living in a developing country, many company heads choose to manage their Vietnam businesses from more Westernized environments. Singapore, because of its proximity to the business hub of Ho Chi Minh City (only a 1.5 hour flight), is the choice for many. Some expatriate managers base themselves in Singapore and fly into Ho Chi Minh City on Monday morning and return home again on Friday evening after the work week. The inconvenience of the commute is outweighed by the peace of mind that the family is in a comfortable environment.

Managing a business from further away, such as Europe or the United States, presents additional challenges. Vietnam is not a country where you can simply set up a business and then leave it to run itself. If you have an expatriate manager who understands the company culture you are trying to build and the business goals you are trying to achieve, then half the success equation has been achieved. The other half of this equation is how well the manager can function in Vietnam, and how well he can communicate with and manage a Vietnamese team.

If you decide to rely on a local Vietnamese business partner to run your business, then the challenge is managing expectations on both sides. You can't communicate too much in Vietnam; while language is a big barrier, the culture is an even bigger one. The picture in your mind, when you discuss a topic with your partner, will be different from the picture in your partner's mind. The country lacks the business history and evolution that most Western countries have had. What is simple and clear to you may be quite complex and new to your partner. You won't have a similar frame of reference for business concepts. However, once you and your partner have mutual understandings of and agreements about the business, your partner will be very effective in ensuring that the desired outcomes are achieved.

Since the key to success in managing a business from abroad is communication and trust, the foreign partner will have to spend a great deal of time in Vietnam in the early stages of business development and to visit frequently for some time afterward. E-mail and a telephone conversation are great ways to stay in contact between visits, but they can also create opportunities for misunderstandings.

Over-communication is important. Saying something, saying it again and then saying it again in a slightly different way will help your partner to form a picture in his mind that is closer to the one in yours. Over-communicating, building trust, and creating a genuine friendship with your business partner by prioritizing your relationship with him or her above the business itself will ease the inherent difficulties of managing a business in Vietnam without actually being there.

SUMMARY

Partnerships are an important part of doing business in Vietnam. They are required in certain sectors of the economy, and will remain so for the foreseeable future. More important than the requirement for a partnership is their genuine need in order to be successful. A partnership, if structured correctly and built upon a foundation of trust and mutual respect, can yield profound benefits. There are certainly more stories of failure than success with partnerships in Vietnam. The perception of the average Westerner of how business should be conducted is very different from the average Vietnamese. And one cannot impose his or her expectations on the other. A happy compromise must be achieved, and this is something the Vietnamese are adept at.

ENDNOTES

1. "Vietnam's WTO Membership Begins," BBC, January 11, 2007, http://news.bbc.co.uk/1/hi/business/6249705.stm
2. "Working Party on the Accession of Vietnam," Part II Schedule of Specific Commitments in Services, WT/ACC/VNM/48/Add.2, October 27, 2006.
3. Ibid.
4. "Entrepreneurs Unbound," *The Economist*, May 2008, page 8.
5. Ibid.
6. "Joint Ventures Explained," *Contract Journal*, June 6, 2007, Blake Newport Associates, http://www.blakenewport.co.uk/bna-news-and-media.asp?id=18

CHAPTER 7
Legal and Other Administrative Hurdles

Legal compliance and other administrative necessities will command a disproportionate amount of management time in Vietnam. When compared to countries with less bureaucratic governments, Vietnam's requirements are heavy. Recognize this early on and plan to commit resources to address its bureaucracy, permitting regulations and administrative reporting requirements. The systems and the business environment will be uniquely unfamiliar to the expatriate manager. It's easy to get behind and you will need to dedicate massive amounts of time to cleaning up a mess created by not doing things correctly from the start.

Adding to the complexity of the system is its ever-changing nature. New decrees, directives and resolutions are passed regularly and are often unclear. For a small company, keeping abreast of all the changes and remaining in compliance can be very difficult. For a big company, with a more complex business model and larger scale, the system's requirements correspondingly get more stringent.

However, changes are occurring. Different ministries are computerizing their systems. Procedures are being simplified, and outdated processes are being eliminated. A wise business person will do the research and prepare for delays that will require time and resources.

PERMITTING

We interviewed a senior international counsel with British Petroleum (BP), who was with the company in Vietnam from 2001 to late 2006. He is a specialist in oil and gas law and is still with the company, but now based in Singapore. This individual chose to speak with us but remain anonymous. BP has extensive business interests in Vietnam ranging from offshore drilling activity to onshore refinery and power plant facilities. During his time in Vietnam, he estimates that the company was involved in investments totaling over two billion dollars in the country. They operate through several different business units and under numerous structures including 100 percent foreign-owned enterprises and joint ventures. The company's activities in Vietnam are enormous, and typical of the biggest multinationals in the world, but their experience does hint at what can be expected. This legal counsel speaks about some of the permitting requirements that the company had to go through in pursuit of its business interests.

"From our perspective, one of the biggest challenges we had was in trying to determine which permits we needed to get. We had expansive operations in the country ranging from offshore drilling to the pipeline connecting it to a power plant that we had to build. There were a host of permits that we had to get and we even had a permitting department. Their job was just to research the list of permits. The Excel file that served as a database for this was unbelievable. There weren't that many lawyers involved, but there was an entire team that was dedicated to simply trying to understand what permits we needed to get. The issue was that we not only had the national permits, but also local ones and offshore permits. These included ones for drilling and laying the offshore pipeline. We got involved in fishing rights and a host of other issues.

We had a big issue with a resort hotel in Long Hai, which was very close to where our project came onshore. They claimed that our project was interfering with their room occupancy rates. We ended up renting out the entire hotel for a year in 2002. We wanted to avoid any difficulty with the local officials, who were also responsible for granting us permits. So this is what we did to keep it from getting complicated.

Even with the amount of capital that we were bringing into Vietnam, the government wasn't lenient with us on these requirements. We did have a guarantee from the government, at a very senior level, that they would step in and assist in helping us sort out any problems that we encountered, if we filed properly. This helped us avoid any local officials realizing that they could be the tail wagging the dog in any of our projects."

BP expects more issues of this nature, given the scale and sensitivity of the projects it is pursuing, and their case serves as a warning of the administrative hurdles present.

The legal counsel further describes how permits can be used by the government officials as a leveraging tool to get what they want. For example, PetroVietnam, the state-owned oil and gas company, was a joint venture partner with BP in a company established to buy the natural gas that was being recovered offshore and processed. When the project offshore reached production stage, BP had an agreement with PetroVietnam to buy the gas. Unfortunately, the local demand was not yet there by the time the gas was ready to go on stream, and the government did not want to buy gas that the country wasn't yet ready to use.

The government used a permitting issue to hold up the commissioning of the project for six months, which had a very large negative financial impact on BP. Much later, the company discovered that the lack of demand for natural gas in Vietnam, not the permitting issue in question, was the real reason for the government's actions. The permit issue bought PetroVietnam, who had committed to buying the gas, more time. Eventually, the entire amount committed to was paid for, but delivery was not taken until later. In the first year of the agreement, only 60 percent of the gas committed to was taken.

What was the permitting issue in this case? It dealt with a fire certificate for the onshore facility. BP had installed a chemical-based fire retardant system. The government took issue with this and wanted BP to install a water-based system. In the petroleum world this makes no sense because water isn't effective against gas fires. Six months and several million dollars later, the water-based system was installed alongside the chemical one and the permit was granted. The lesson here is that there is always a reason for seemingly illogical behavior in Vietnam. They are just as rational and business savvy as their counterparts in the West, and perhaps more so.

REGULATION AND OVERALL EASE OF DOING BUSINESS

Vietnam ranks 91 out of 178 countries on the World Bank's 2008 Ease of Doing Business rankings. It has moved up in the rankings by one place from 2007. Its neighbors on the list include the Seychelles and Moldova; last on the list is the Congo, and first is Singapore. The rankings are based on important and broad measurements such as how easy it is to start a business, dealing with licenses, employing workers, registering property, getting credit, paying taxes and trading across borders. These are important criteria in the assessment of the business climate of any country.

It is well known where the country is coming from and the base from which it is improving upon. More important is where Vietnam is going, and how fast it is improving. Where is it going? It was not recognized as a top reformer in 2008. Countries that were recognized include Egypt, which was the top performer, as well as Croatia, Kenya and China. Vietnam was recognized for strengthening investor protections and easing access to credit. But beyond this, not a great deal was done to facilitate the ease with which business can be conducted in the country.[1]

There is a lot of rhetoric in the local media clearly outlining the vastness of the bureaucratic system and huge burden that companies must undertake in order to do business in the country. The changes are slow however, and often when one process is improved, another becomes more onerous.

The most recent issue of concern in the business community is the change in the Personal Income Tax (PIT) law, which was supposed to have come into effect in January 2009, but still seems to be evolving due to contention over its structure. Directives and amendments are being issued to clarify exactly what the new regimen will be.

Under Official Letter No. 42/BTC-TCT of the Ministry of Finance on with-holding personal income tax on sale of securities, dated January 2, 2009, an individual earning income on the sale of securities is no longer exempt from PIT. This in effect places a capital gains tax on stock sales.[2] It is hard to tell what is "firm" and what is still being determined in terms of the details of the PIT tax regime. Like much about doing business in the country, it's hard to tell if you are in compliance or not. Directives are constantly being issued and amendments made. In the case of PIT, a large proportion of these directives are aimed at trying to clarify exactly what the new regime will be.

A lot of effort has to be put into just keeping up with the changes that are supposed to ease the burden on businesses.

Another example occurred on January 1, 2009, when a new unemployment insurance law (social insurance in Vietnam), came into effect. Unemployment insurance is one of the benefits that companies are required to provide to their employees. The former law dates back to 2006. Just a few weeks before the new law came into effect, the government issued Decree 127 to provide the details for the new regimen.

THE POST OFFICE METAPHOR

The post office in Vietnam provides a great metaphor for how administrative procedures are handled on the ground level. The concept of a "queue" hasn't come to Vietnam yet, and postal clerks will generally recognize the loudest or pushiest patron, over those who are first in line. Whoever commands the attention of the clerk most effectively gets his needs taken care of first. And a particularly demanding customer can quite easily divert a postal clerk from the task at hand. The end effect is, of course, that it takes everyone much longer to get served as the clerks are forced to handle multiple tasks at one time.

Some of the other government organizations have gotten past this form of inefficiency and taken things to an entirely new level. Anyone doing business in Vietnam long enough is going to need to go to a government organization at some point or other. Eventually something will need to be translated, or a visa will need to be renewed or some other document will need an official red stamp on it from a particular government department.

Thankfully, there is a keen awareness at very senior levels in the People's Committee that bureaucracy is stifling growth and burdening businesses. Processes are being streamlined and redundant steps are being eliminated. The best way to avoid the frustration altogether is to have a local staff member visit the relevant government office on your behalf. This will usually require a letter of introduction, which is easy enough to generate and saves a huge amount of time.

Laws You Have Probably Already Broken

There are a myriad of laws on the books, which range from the ridiculous and impossible to enforce to the downright scary because the consequences are so severe. Most people don't know about them, and many would laugh if you told them they were breaking the law.

- Color photocopiers, as of July 9, 2008, are strictly regulated and must be approved by government authorities. A special import permit from the Ministry of Information and Communication (MOIC) must be obtained before bringing them in, and registration on the intention to use the photocopier must be made with the local Department of Information and Communication (DOIC). This is all outlined in Circular 04/2008, Decree 105.[3] Pretty serious sounding stuff, which is also very confusing considering the fact that normal black and white printers face no regulation at all. Why all the fuss? It seems that the authorities are worried about a recent increase in counterfeiting activities. There are still a large number of businesses that have color copiers being used daily and are completely unaware of this law.

- Related to this law is Decree No. 97/2008/ND-CP on the management, provision and use of internet services and electronic information on the internet. This decree was made on August 28, 2008, and is the first update in almost seven years to the law governing internet activity.

  The basic update to the old regulation is the differentiation between a "website" and a "general website." A website is loosely defined as a site or combination of sites that facilitate the supply and exchange of information. A general website is defined as a site that supplies information on politics, economics, culture and society by citing information from official sources, press agencies, or websites of the Party or other state agencies. Because of the sensitivity, these general websites are required to get a special license from the MOIC.

  Yahoo! Vietnam recently drew attention for its activities on the internet in Vietnam. The company currently only has a Representative Office License, which prohibits them from conducting business activities in Vietnam. But Yahoo! has a site (www.yahoo.com.vn) that has products including email, chat and news services that directly target the Vietnamese market. Operating in this gray area has drawn the attention of the company's competitors.[4]

  The general manager of Yahoo! Vietnam explained the law. It was noted that websites that end in ".vn" are subject to control by the MOIC, but websites that end in .com, are not. The lesson here is to tread carefully, as cyberspace is a gray area still, with much being open to interpretation.

- You are required to have your passport with you when you fly in Vietnam, even domestically. This isn't a big deal for travelers, but if you are living in the country it is easy to forget. You can provide a photocopy sometimes, but you have to push extremely hard; the substitution has to be approved by airport security, which takes time. You are also required to present your passport at hotels. The big, international hotels will simply photocopy your passport and return it to you; smaller hotels will try to keep it until your departure. The hotels are required to "register" you as a guest in their hotel with the local police department. It's actually against U.S. law to turn your passport over to a third party. It is considered U.S. property and legally can only be turned over to a representative of the U.S. government.

• Watch out for a change in the law on advertising. Supposedly coming into effect sometime in 2009 is a law limiting the amount of space that can be dedicated to advertising on a website (10 percent).

• As detailed earlier in this chapter, changes to the Personal Income Tax (PIT) law, means that an individual earning income on the sale of securities is no longer exempt from PIT.[5]

ENDNOTES

1. "2008 World Bank EoDB Rankings: Comparing Regulations in 178 Economies," World Bank, pages 3, 9.
2. "Vietnam Legal Update," Allens Arthur Robinson, January 2009, page 1.
3. Ibid, page 11.
4. Ibid, page 9.
5. Ibid, page 1.

PART 3

The Daily Challenges—Go!

CHAPTER 8

Manufacturing, Outsourcing, and Agricultural Production

Two compelling attractions for setting up business in Vietnam are the cost of labor and the country's high literacy rate. Companies have entered Vietnam over the past decade to capitalize on the cheap labor force by having their products manufactured there. Vietnam serves as an alternative to China for those companies seeking production diversity and less vulnerability to becoming over-reliant on just one country for production. Big players are coming into the country with massive investments, and the trend will probably continue.

Vietnam is being pursued for the outsourcing potential that a well-educated and literate workforce offers. This is a recent phenomenon; as the business environment matures in the big cities, it is producing a more developed pool of talent for hire, particularly in the IT sector. Companies are setting up shop, mostly in Ho Chi Minh City, and are typically foreign-run but capitalizing on the large pool of local talent and low wages.

Unquestionably, the most impressive sector of Vietnam's growth over the past couple of decades has been its farming and agricultural industry. In the mid 1980s, a brief experiment with farm collectivism brought famine to the country, but by 2000 Vietnam was the number two worldwide exporter of Robusta coffee as well as rice, second only to Colombia and Thailand. Vietnam has had significant success in producing other agricultural commodities including nuts, peppers, rubber, and tea. Vietnam is also a large exporter of seafood and timber. In 2007, Vietnam's farm, timber and fisheries industries grew by 21 percent to $12.5 billion, with further gains in 2008.[1]

MANUFACTURING IN VIETNAM

Vietnam is particularly interested in high-valued investment projects. The country wants large amounts of foreign capital flowing into the country, and thus focuses its efforts on licensing big manufacturing projects. Smaller projects with lower amounts of capital face more hurdles in licensing and receive little to no incentives for coming into the country. Manufacturing tends to be capital-intensive and Vietnam welcomes foreign investors into this space.

Taiwan is one of the largest foreign investor countries into Vietnam. As the Association of South East Asian Nations (ASEAN) has progressed towards a free trade zone (FTZ) for its members, Taiwanese companies have flooded into Vietnam to set up plants and take advantage of the huge markets this will give them preferential access to. By 2015, the ten-member nation and 550 million consumers-strong ASEAN hopes to have a FTZ formed which would allow for the unrestricted movement of trade, capital, services and labor between the members. ASEAN members include Brunei Dar a-Salaam, Cambodia, Indonesia, Laos, Malaysia, Myanmar, the Philippines, Singapore, Thailand and Vietnam. The most recent wave of Vietnam-bound investment from Taiwan has targeted the manufacturing of industrial materials and hi-tech products. Companies such as China Steel, Formosa Plastics and Acer Group (the PC manufacturer), are just some of the industrial giants that plan to expand or begin manufacturing operations in the huge industrial zones being developed in Vietnam.[2]

Hon Hai Precision, the world's largest electronics manufacturing service provider, is investing $5 billion to set up an industrial zone in Vinh Phu province that will cover over 1,000 hectares. Formosa Plastics is investing $8 billion to build a mega steel plant.[3]

Big American names are also present or are entering the manufacturing space. Nike's suppliers have been producing shoes under the Nike brand name in Vietnam for over a decade, and it is the company's largest supplier of footwear worldwide. The subcontractors that supply Nike with shoes and apparel employ 130,000 people in Vietnam.[4] We had a chance to interview Amanda Tucker, a former general manager of Nike in Vietnam. Nike has an established presence in the country for over a decade now and Amanda was able to give us some insight into the company's reasons for producing in Vietnam, challenges the company faces and what it has been able to accomplish since it began operations.

BV: How long were you with Nike in Vietnam and in what capacity? What were your title and job responsibilities/objectives?

AT: I was in Vietnam for three years, from July 2004–July 2007, as general manager. I oversaw our footwear operations in Vietnam. My main objective was to ensure that our contract factories met our quality, CR, and production standards. When I arrived in Vietnam we were exporting roughly 52 million pairs of shoes out of Vietnam per year. When I left, our production exports had grown to approximately 75 million pairs of shoes per year.

BV: How long has Nike been manufacturing through its suppliers in Vietnam?

AT: We began operations in Vietnam in 1995.

BV: Why did Nike and its suppliers choose to commit so much production to Vietnam?

AT: We have had a good business environment in Vietnam. We've had room (physically) to expand there, and have been happy with the quality of the product coming out of Vietnam. The country is politically stable and there is an ample supply of labor. The Government has been historically willing to work with foreign investors.

BV: What makes the country so appealing over competing alternatives, beyond the obviously cheap labor and literate workforce?

AT: I would say that the workforce is very motivated and has a strong work ethic.

BV: What pitfalls has Nike encountered in Vietnam? What should a business manager be on the lookout for?

AT: A business manager in Vietnam must always be aware of the pitfalls of corruption. He/she must stay vigilant to ensure that the company's core values are maintained. Vietnam is also facing severe constraints in terms of infrastructure (roads, ports) and this will increasingly impact, especially the manufacturing sector.

BV: Are there any particulars to manufacturing in Vietnam, versus other countries, that one should be aware of?

AT: My main concern here would be the infrastructure issues I've mentioned above. In the absence of an effective approach to the mediation of labor disputes, wildcat strikes will continue to be a concern.

Intel, in late 2006, decided to build the world's largest chip assembly and testing plant in Vietnam. The chip plant is set to be built outside of Ho Chi Minh City covering 500,000 square feet, and it will employ more than 4,000 workers. This is the first semiconductor facility to be built in the country and it represented the single largest foreign investment at the time of licensing in 2006. Intel cited several reasons for choosing Vietnam over other potential countries. These reasons included an increasing attention to the education system in the country, a strong workforce and a forward-looking government.[5] This is where the government's focus is, and this is the kind of massive investment that is coming into the country.

QUALITY CONCERNS

One of the primary concerns in manufacturing in Vietnam is product quality. Newly emergent manufacturing destinations typically have problems with quality control, which can be attributed to the challenges of setting up a business in a new country and the lack of focus on quality in the early stages of operations. Training of staff is typically a long-term endeavor; it takes time to bring the workforce up to a certain level. The quality of the machinery and technology is also a concern in new manufacturing ventures. Companies like to commit in stages; first by focusing on lower-value production that allows for lower quality, and later bringing in expensive equipment, quality control systems and more sophisticated training after the destination has proven itself viable as a long-term manufacturing location.

Nike's strategy in Vietnam is an example of how companies target low-wage countries for low-value manufacturing and slowly increase the quality standards and complexity of the products being produced as the workforce and infrastructure develop. Nike originally sourced its shoes from factories in Taiwan and Korea. As the wage rates in these countries escalated, Nike moved much of its low-end production to Vietnam, China, Indonesia and other low-wage countries. In 1995, a Korean company (one of Nike's major production partners) opened the first manufacturing facility for Nike shoes. In the early stages of production in Vietnam, Nike focused on manufacturing low-priced and less technologically complicated shoes and apparel. Taiwan and Korea continued to manufacture the products that required the most complex technology and more sensitive brand secrets. As time has gone on, more complicated shoe models have slowly been moved into Vietnam. The country wants the higher-valued production because it increases the GDP of the country and enables the factories to pay higher wages. It is just one of the many steps that bring economic development, higher paying jobs and a better living for its people.

STRIKES

The labor market in Vietnam is not static. With the boom in new manufacturing jobs in Vietnam has come the inevitable rise in worker discontent. Wage rates are rising rapidly in the country, but not fast enough to outpace the rate of inflation in 2007 and 2008, or the aspirations of a young and dynamic workforce for a better life. There is constant pressure to increase wages to both compensate for inflation, and satiate the increasing appetite of the population for newly available consumer goods.

In April of 2008, Nike was at the forefront of labor issues with 20,000 employees going on strike at a Taiwanese-owned factory that makes shoes for the footwear company. The owner of the factory is irrelevant. Nike got the bad press because it's a global brand with vast media appeal. The dispute centered on the workers demand for a 20 percent increase in pay to their $59 monthly salaries. This is indicative of the wave of labor discontent that is washing over the country.

In 2007, there were 541 labor disputes that resulted in strikes across the country. The disputes involved approximately 350,000 workers. Many of the companies involved in these strikes are the same ones that the Communist-led government has worked hard to entice into the country, which puts the government into both an ironic and precarious position. The current Communist government was founded upon a mass revolutionary movement; however, its current legitimacy depends on its ability to push forward the economic reforms and maintain the high rates of growth it has promised. The rising tide of labor disputes threatens to undermine this.[6]

It is no secret that companies are choosing to manufacture in Vietnam because it is cheap. The more expensive it gets, relative to other country options, the less attractive it becomes. When cheap labor markets disappear, so do foreign investors. Many of the countries that once hosted large manufacturing industries, such as Japan, Korea and Taiwan, are now the owners of large manufacturing businesses overseas. All of these countries started out as very attractive bases for manufacturing before they moved upscale into higher-valued and more technical product manufacturing, and before they went abroad with their expertise. If Vietnam is to realize the full benefits of having a modernized market and better-paying jobs in the future, it needs to maintain the attractiveness of its current market. Labor disputes and onerous labor laws could undermine its current appeal to foreign investors.

TAX INCENTIVES

Vietnam, like other countries in Southeast Asia, wants large manufacturing-intensive industries that create a high number of jobs and bring huge sums of capital into the country. In order to remain competitive, the country has had to match the incentives that other countries in the region have offered, including tax holidays of up to eight years, reduced corporate income tax rates, accelerated rates of depreciation, special exemptions from import duties and exemptions on other indirect taxes. These incentives are focused almost exclusively on foreign investors, exporters and investments into the poorer regions of the country.[7]

It's important to note that these incentives are only available to foreign-invested projects that meet certain criteria. For example, a foreign company can receive a refund of up to 100 percent of its corporate income taxes if it reinvests all of its profits for three consecutive years in the country. The corporate income tax rate in Vietnam is quite high at 28 percent, so receiving tax incentives is important. It may even be the deciding factor in whether a company decides to invest in Vietnam or not. Exemptions from import duties and value added tax (VAT) are also limited to certain sectors. It's not a given that a company will qualify, and as stated before, the larger the proposed investment the better a company's chance of receiving incentives.

OUTSOURCING TO VIETNAM

When one thinks of outsourcing, what typically come to mind are places like India, South Korea and China. India in particular, has built a reputation for IT outsourcing along with huge high-tech parks and an education system focused on developing engineers and programmers. Vietnam hardly ranks as a name one would consider when asked to list the top hotspots for budding IT development around the world. Microsoft, however, and a host of the other top global names in the information technology business consider Vietnam a viable host country.

In 2002, Microsoft outsourced some of the design work for the "Forza-Motorsport" video game that comes on the company's Xbox game console. A very small outfit named Glass Egg Digital, based in Ho Chi Minh City, was one of the participants in a pilot project to design cars for the popular video game, and after impressing the right people at Microsoft, the relationship between the two companies has grown. Currently, Glass Egg does nearly all of the design work for the 330 different models of cars that are used in the video game and will soon begin working on the considerably more difficult task of actually designing the tracks and the cities through which the cars race. This Vietnam-based design firm has met Microsoft's quality standards, and the two companies are increasing the scope of their business relationship. The video gaming industry is a bigger market, in terms of gross revenue, than the movie industry and is a huge part of Microsoft's business.

Other big names that have found the right mix of high quality and low prices for outsourcing to Vietnam in the IT sector include Electronic Arts, Sony Computer Entertainment Europe, Codemasters, Atari, Nortel, Comsys and Alcatel-Lucent. And Glass Egg isn't the only player in the game. There are others who are competing for a piece of this lucrative IT pie. Alive Interactive is a key competitor of Glass Egg, and TMA Solutions have been successful in attracting software development work as well.[8]

The country has proven successful in a very short period of time at carving out a niche in the IT industry. The types of jobs and technology entering the country give a major boost to the living standards of the workforce.

Quality Concerns

Even smaller players are coming to Vietnam to get their IT work outsourced. Seth Restaino, who works as a senior web producer in the United States and has been in the industry for over 15 years, has this to say about his experience in outsourcing work to a company called District 3 in Ho Chi Minh City.

"We chose to outsource the development of a number of our web-based properties to a Vietnamese team based in Ho Chi Minh City. The team has the skill set we wanted and was willing and able to come up to speed quickly on a technology we use—called a MVC (model-view-controller) system—that is built on top of technologies with which they were already familiar.

Their references were great, their estimates are consistently in line with our expectations, and perhaps most importantly they are agile and roll with the punches. They have a start-up mentality and a get-it-done attitude, which dovetails nicely with our team's personality and modus operandi.

Finally, communication has been excellent. We work directly with an American project manager based over there, as well as a Vietnamese technical lead who speaks fluent English, and there have been no communication breakdowns to speak of. Subtleties are understood."

All of this praise for the outstanding quality the country has exhibited in IT outsourcing does need a word of caution, however. Intellectual property rights are a real concern, as is outlined elsewhere in this book. Property is not viewed the same way here. Ample precautions should be taken to protect your interests. Pirated copies of videos and software can readily be found on the streets and back-alley markets. Even well-paid software engineers and designers can be tempted, particularly in an environment where, although their jobs are good, they are still being used because they are cheaper than their counterparts in other countries.

Education and Literacy

Education is highly valued in Vietnam. The country has one of the highest rates of adult literacy in all of Southeast Asia, with 95 percent for men and 91 percent for women. The roots of this exceptional rate of literacy for such a poor country go back to the Confucian philosophy embraced by much of the country and the commitments made by political leaders on September 8, 1945, when Ho Chi Minh launched the first campaign for the eradication of illiteracy. Between 1990 and 2000, the country made an even more ambitious statement of its priorities by setting up committees for literacy in every province, district and village in the entire country.

To be deemed literate in Vietnam, a person must pass a standardized national exam, which targets the literacy levels expected of a 3rd to 5th grader in primary school. By comparison, in Thailand, literacy is based on whether a person can read a simple sentence in a newspaper.[9] So the literacy rate in Vietnam is high in both percentage terms and quality. This emphasis on basic education gives the labor force a firm base upon which to grow and enables the labor force to be malleable and for knowledge to be easily transferable. Generally speaking, the workforce is prepared for, and welcomes, learning opportunities.

Companies that have a vested interest in a highly-educated workforce are contributing to the education system in Vietnam. They are developing relationships with the local universities in order to influence curriculum, and they are helping to fund and sponsor scholarships to top students who may prove to be prospective employees. BP sponsors the Chevening Scholarship, which provides for top students to pursue postgraduate degrees in the United Kingdom.

Companies are finding a well-established base from which to develop a pool of talent. Seth Restaino, who commented earlier on the high level of quality he has found in the outsourcing of certain IT functions, had this to say about his reasons for considering the country and ultimately choosing it over other competitive markets.

> Vietnam is attractive to us because it has experienced an economic renaissance in the last decade, and one contributing factor may be the strength of its educational system in terms of preparing Vietnamese citizens for the global workforce. The number of qualified English-speaking web developers in Vietnam, and the organization and availability thereof, has been eye-opening. The Vietnamese team we're working with is both professional and eager to grow with us, and I think that's probably a reflection of their preparation. Vietnam seems to be doing it right.

However, there are some differences in the educational philosophy and history between North and South Vietnam. In 1954, when Vietnam was divided by the war, the South pursued a system similar to the U.S., while the North pursued a system of mass education based on the theories of Marx and Lenin. When the country was reunified in 1975, the communist system of education spread throughout the entire country. The emphasis on technological training is seen as equal in importance to that of teaching communist ideas. It also may explain why Ho Chi Minh City in the South, has developed into the business hub of the country, while Hanoi in the North, is clearly the political hub.[10]

Partially because of this history, companies are finding that although the level of technical knowledge and aptitude is high in the country, the soft skill knowledge base in the labor force is notably low. People can easily be brought up to speed and trained in a certain segment of the workforce, but are sorely lacking the skills that are needed to organize, plan, manage, and lead at a supervisory level. Aidan Lynam, the CEO of Holcim Cement, notes in an interview that the technical skills of a group of workers he was responsible for training, was "off the chart." It was the soft skills that were lacking. His staff was unable to problem-solve, supervise or lead when the real-life situations presented themselves.

In response to this obvious lack in a critical skill set, two things have happened. The first is that companies have had to fill mid-level management positions with expatriates, instead of locals. The second is that there has been a boom in corporate training organizations that have come into the country to help fill this void. These corporate training companies are attempting to fill the soft skill gaps, rather than the hard skills, by focusing their programs around themes such as leadership, communication, problem solving, time management, creativity and team building. Even established programs such as RMIT University's MBA program have begun to look at supplementing the traditional curriculum for an MBA with these soft skills. And the number of team-building companies based in the country has exploded in the past decade, from just a couple, to dozens that specialize in these services.

AGRICULTURAL PRODUCTION

Vietnam's agriculture, farming and fisheries industries provide about half of the jobs in all of Vietnam. This is down considerably over the past few years as development has brought many people from the countryside to the cities. However, 70 percent of the population still lives in the countryside, and these industries, although decreasing in percentage of total gross domestic product, are still growing and essential to a healthy development of the country.

In the late 1980s, Vietnam's government reversed its collectivist policies, in which land was taken from the people, and gave the land back. At the same time, Vietnam began to liberalize, rather than control, farm prices and embarked on an increasingly open trade policy. This allowed for the country to take full advantage of its abundant natural resources and fertile land and its low-cost labor force to work it. The country has made improvements in the productivity of its farmers by encouraging the consolidation of farms, which provided for increased economies of scale, and a worker productivity rate that surpasses that of China, India, Indonesia, Thailand, the Philippines and Malaysia.[11]

Foreign-run companies have come into this market segment with success as well. A particularly good example is a very successful flower farm (choosing to remain anonymous), which established itself in 1994 in the highlands of Dalat in Lam Dong province. The company decided to take advantage of the temperate climate in Lam Dong province by focusing on cut flowers and cool-weather crops. In 1996, the company branched out into the dairy and vegetable markets by acquiring a local farm through a joint venture, which was eventually bought out and is now 100 percent foreign-owned. Interestingly, the joint venture partner that was bought out was paid in cows.

Today, this company produces 65 million flower stems a year, is the largest cut flower farm in Asia and one of the biggest in the world with 55 hectares under cultivation. The company does $18 million in sales, has 1,200 employees and has experienced consistent growth of between 15–20 percent since it began operations well over a decade ago. Twenty-eight percent of the company's production is sold into the domestic market, and the other 72 percent is sold into markets such as Japan, Taiwan, Singapore and Australia. To say the company has been successful in Vietnam would be an understatement.

We had the chance to interview a senior level Dutch manager at the company in October of 2008. This individual, who chose to remain anonymous, has been with the company for five years in his current capacity, but was initially a project manager for seven years. The manager cites three main reasons for Vietnam's desirability in the cut flower market. The first reason is the climate. Dalat and Lam Dong province, at 1,400 meters in elevation, are cool year-round, which is very good for the cool-weather crops the company grows. The second reason is the labor, both in terms of price and quality. Labor rates are low, even when compared with other Asian countries, and the workforce has proven to be very trainable and productive. The location of Vietnam and the logistical requirements of the business also made Vietnam desirable. Flowers often have a very short shelf life, and, because the country is geographically close to many of its markets, the company is able to get its product to market in an efficient manner. The manager also noted that the country is easier to get important equipment into than other countries, which has helped his labor force be more productive and has lowered the company's unit costs.

This manager also cited three main reasons why the company initially chose Vietnam to establish and grow its business over other Asian countries. The company had looked at other Southeast Asian countries, and had business interests in Indonesia, before deciding to focus exclusively on Vietnam. The first reason was political climate and ease of doing business. Vietnam is more politically stable than a country like the Philippines, and is easier to do business in than China. Weather risk has also been a strong contributing factor. The inland central highlands of Vietnam are less vulnerable to the hurricanes and other big storms that other countries experience. Finally, when compared to other countries, including Indonesia for example, Lam Dong has a cooler and more stable temperature because it is further away from the equator.

It's important to note that the company is not located in a big commercial hub or city. The Vietnam government wants to promote business in outlying and less-developed parts of the country, so the company was able to secure preferential tax treatment, paying no taxes for the first five years of operations and then moving to a 10 percent tax rate. The senior manager we interviewed noted that this tax treatment is locked in for the farm, but probably not available for new companies coming into the country.

Finally, and probably most important, when asked about the most pressing things for a businessman coming into the country to be aware of, he explained the biggest mistakes that people make are: 1) a lack of understanding of the laws and regulations; 2) a lack of focus on public relations with the government with a goal of establishing relationships with key contacts; and 3) a lack of protocol and using the correct channels to go through to get things done. Failure to prioritize these things makes executives and businesses less effective and adds significantly to the cost and time taken to establish a business. These are the mistakes that are most common to expatriate business people because they are the concepts most foreign to them.

SUMMARY

Vietnam has attracted a great deal of investment in its manufacturing, outsourcing and agricultural sectors. A low-cost and well-educated labor force has been credited with much of the interest of foreign companies. It's important to understand how the labor force evolved into its current "shape" as well as how it is further changing. The real value in moving into a country like Vietnam is not in the ability to take advantage of the low cost of labor, but rather in how to effectively increase its productivity and improve the quality of the goods and services it generates. A mutually beneficial situation occurs in which the company benefits from higher quality products that it can sell for a better price, and the country benefits through an increase in living standards driven by higher productivity and wages.

ENDNOTES

1. "From Basket Case to Rice Basket," May 2, 2008, *The Economist*, page 10.
2. "ASEAN Free Trade Zone Turning Vietnam Into Major Factory Base for Taiwan," August 26, 2008, www.cens.com (*Taiwan Economic News*), http://www.cens.com/cens/html/en/news/news_inner_24438.html

3. Ibid.

4. "Good Morning Vietnam," March 13, 2006, www.businessweek.com, http://www.businessweek.com/magazine/content/06_11/b3975068.htm

5. "Intel to Invest $1 Billion in Vietnam as Country Strives to Raise Hi-tech Profile," November 18, 2006, www.usatoday.com, http://www.usatoday.com/tech/news/2006-11-18-vietnam_x.htm

6. "Labor Versus Market in Vietnam," April 5, 2008, Asia Times Online, http://www.atimes.com/atimes/Southeast_Asia/JD05Ae02.html

7. Kevin Fletcher, "Tax Incentives in Cambodia, Lao PDR, and Vietnam," International Monetary Fund Conference on Foreign Direct Investment, August 16, 2002.

8. "Vietnam's Growing Role in Outsourcing," December 11, 2006, BusinessWeek.com, http://www.businessweek.com/technology/content/dec2006/tc20061211_099877.htm

9. "On Course Towards Full Literacy," September 8, 2002, www.unesco.org, http://portal.unesco.org/education/en/ev.php-URL_ID=8518&URL_DO=DO_TOPIC&URL_SECTION=201.html

10. "Education/Literacy in Vietnam," asianinfo.org, http://www.asianinfo.org/asianinfo/vietnam/pro-education.htm

11. "From Basket Case to Rice Basket," May 2, 2008, *The Economist*, pages 10, 11.

CHAPTER 9
Selling into the Vietnamese Market

The Vietnamese marketplace has radically changed over the past 10 years. The standard of living has increased dramatically in a very short time. In the decade from 1996 to 2006 the gross domestic product of the country has grown from $24.7 billion to $59.3 billion, and gross national income in the three short years from 2003 to 2006 grew from $470 billion to $690 billion.[1] What does this mean? People now have more disposable income than in recent history, and the rate of growth is much faster than anywhere in the West. People are consuming at a faster rate, and in a country of 85 million people, this presents some amazing opportunities to provide products that were previously unavailable or unaffordable.

Many companies have gone into the Vietnamese market to take advantage of the relatively cheap and well-educated labor force, but many are also seeing the growing opportunity to sell into the country. Vietnam is not one market with one distinct profile. Long-time expatriates in Vietnam note that Hanoi and Ho Chi Minh City have very different cultures. In Hanoi, the arts matter and people relax for hours smoking, drinking tea and reading poetry. In Ho Chi Minh City, where the brand of motorbike you drive and the price of your cell phone are the determining factors of status, the locals drink coffee and talk business. The country is over 1,600 kilometers long, and the sales and marketing strategies that work in Ho Chi Minh City might not prove as successful in Hanoi.

WHAT THE VIETNAMESE WANT

Cell phones are popular in Vietnam, with 8 million units sold in 2008 and projected mobile phone sales reaching $1 billion. The growth rate isn't slowing down, with double the number of cell phones being sold compared to two years ago.[2] This rapid adoption of technology makes looking at the mobile telecom market a must in studying "what works" in the retail space of this country.

Nokia was one of the early movers in Vietnam, gaining a huge share of the market very early on and maintaining that lead until today. Nokia was so successful that up until very recently, the model of cell phone was considered a reflection of your social standing; people would spend a large percentage of their monthly income to possess the newest Nokia model, even though many of the features were fairly useless to them. People saw the cell phone as an "investment" in their social status.

How did Nokia manage to deliver such impressive sales results in a country that was still quite poor at the beginning of the 21st century? The first thing they did was to identify a need. Vietnam lacked a good telecommunications infrastructure. Most people didn't have a telephone in their homes because the country wasn't wired for it. If they did have a home phone, the service was usually poor. Nokia saw this as an opportunity to "leap frog" the old technology with a new solution. This got Nokia into the market.

The next step was less logical and far more strategic and calculating. Most of the phones that Nokia sold early on in Vietnam were not the kind of low-end, budget cell phones often sold in a developing country. On the contrary, Nokia managed to immediately turn the cell phone into a status symbol. They didn't go in and saturate the market with cheap phones. Instead, they marketed at the high end of the product range to the need, which Nokia correctly identified as function *and* status. Nokia embarked on an aggressive advertising campaign in the early days that played on people's desires to have Western things and to be modern and new. TV commercials, print ads and posters all clearly outlined the high profile life that came with a Nokia phone.

Nokia's answer to the question of what the Vietnamese want might be: "Exactly what you tell them they want." The Vietnamese didn't know what they wanted in terms of products and services because they didn't know what was available. This is changing rapidly, but Vietnamese people are often more easily marketed to than people in the West. In America, the marketing has been intense for so long now that people are desensitized to it. It takes more sophisticated and creative ideas to get people's attention. In Vietnam, people are being marketed to for the first time. Nokia, as an early mover in a market still sensitive to advertising, got an incredible bang for their marketing buck.

More recently, things have changed in the cell phone market. Dinh Anh Huan, the business director at Vietnam's largest cell phone retailer, the Gioi Di Dong, notes that the downward trend in cell phone prices is being driven by a change in perception. "Cell phones are no longer considered signs of social status as they previously have been," he said.[3] Last year, Nokia Vietnam introduced a series of cell phone products to target rural consumers. This shift in marketing strategy, in response to the realization that the product was being commoditized at the lower end, has resulted in Nokia increasing its market share by 10 percent and maintaining its number one position. Recently they have faced intense competition from other market entrants such as Samsung, Motorola and Sony Ericsson.

In 2009, per commitments made through the World Trade Organization, the cell phone retail market will open. Previously, Nokia had used local distributors to sell into the country. With this requirement no longer in place, the company could feasibly sell directly to the consumer.

Motorbikes are another interesting product. You can't cross the street in Ho Chi Minh City without feeling like you're in a real life rendition of the video game "Frogger." In the 1990s, as the country began to slowly awake from its post-war slumber, and the big cities started to court foreign investment, the need for a means of transportation, other than a pedal bike, arose. Interestingly though, the market for this product has done the opposite of what was seen in the cell phone market. Cheap models of the motorbike were the first to be adopted by the market.

The Honda "Dream" was the early product of choice for the average Vietnamese, and people were proud to own one. Chinese versions of the Honda, that are even cheaper, were also extremely popular. High-end versions of the motorbike, like the Italian-made Piaggio ET8 and Vespa scooters did not become popular until much later. Instead of becoming commoditized, the motorbike evolved into a status symbol. Part of the reason for this might be due to the price. While a high-end cell phone may only cost $200 to $300, a high-end motorbike is more in the range of $4,000 to $6,000. Something can't be turned into a status symbol unless a meaningful segment of the market can afford it.

Examining the market for motorbikes in Vietnam a little deeper yields some other interesting insights. Piaggio is not a new entrant to the Vietnamese market. Old, classic versions of the Vespa 150 Sprint and Lambretta were very common sights on the streets of any southern Vietnamese city until a few years ago. Now they are much less common as most have either been exported out of the country, or rebuilt and "tricked out" by the youth looking to be cool and trendy. The old classic motorbikes were exported because the price they command abroad was markedly higher than what they would fetch in the country. The Vietnamese don't want old vestiges of the past; they want the newest and latest. The word "classic" doesn't hold value for them; classic means old. A classic Vespa from the 1960s that would fetch $200 in Ho Chi Minh City a few years ago can cost several thousand dollars, depending on how rare it is, once refurbished in either the U.S. or Europe. One young Vietnamese office worker, when questioned about her purchase of a new Piaggio, which took several years to save up for, sums up the appeal of the brand by saying, "When I ride a Piaggio, I feel more confident."[4]

Other segments of the consumer market are showing the same trends. New, higher-end shopping centers are going up in both Ho Chi Minh City and Hanoi, and existing spaces in the malls that have already been built are commanding a premium. Rents have risen from $30/$36 a square meter in 2005 to over $60 per square meter in 2008. An American company is developing an eight-screen cinema in Vincom City Towers taking up over

4,000 square meters of space to cater to people's developing tastes for Western-style entertainment.[5]

You can't help but wonder how a country that is still quite poor is able to afford these luxuries. Two partial answers to the question are 1) the 7 percent economic growth rate the country has experienced over the past few years, and 2) the $3 billion dollars a year in foreign remittances that the country receives.[6] Many of the Vietnamese boat people who fled the country after the fall of Saigon in 1975 regularly send money into the country to family and friends who were "left behind." These two factors contribute a great deal of wealth to the growing middle class.

BRANDING AND NAME RECOGNITION

The demand for the "new" means a demand for those brands that are well known in the West, as these were previously not available. The Vietnamese are very aware of the top brands in a broad spectrum of product categories. Gucci, Rolex, Prada and Armani are all brands that the average urban Vietnamese knows. However, this doesn't mean that if you aren't selling a well-branded product you can't sell into Vietnam. A number of local companies have successfully built up their brands within the country, and a couple have expanded to do business abroad.

Vietnam is the second largest coffee exporting country in the world and the largest exporter of Robusta coffee. There is a very distinct coffee culture in the country, which has developed since the French first introduced the stimulant. One local company has taken advantage of this strength and built up a formidable brand name. Trung Nguyen coffee shops can be seen in almost any city in Vietnam and are probably more prevalent than Starbucks is in the West.

Trung Nguyen used a franchise model to overcome the large financial obstacle of building a recognized brand. The company was the first to apply the franchise model on a large scale and used it to grow from a few shops in 1998 to over 1,000 in 2006.[7] They were able to capitalize on the "big city" image that the brand carried early on and translate this into a business model that made the company's brand name recognized throughout the country.

Trung Nguyen's business model and brand have become so successful that the company has been able to take its business global by opening shops in the U.S., China, Singapore and Japan. The new shop in Singapore's Changi International Airport is the first of its kind to pursue a uniquely Vietnamese look and style.[8] Previous coffee shops outside of Vietnam pursued more of a Western style and feel which put them in direct competition with the likes of Starbucks and other global coffee giants. The strategy capitalizes on the company's origin and roots. The franchise model is still being employed by Trung Nguyen today, but the branding that a franchisee gets, along with the support in terms of store design and atmosphere, have been enhanced. This attempt to become a competitive brand in the world coffee market shows that it isn't imperative to be an established brand before entering the Vietnamese market; brands can and have been built from nothing. The Vietnamese are a proud people. They would happily buy a Vietnamese brand if the perceived quality of that brand met the same standards as its foreign competitors.

Another emerging brand name in Vietnam is Highlands Coffee. This company pursued a very different strategy to Trung Nguyen and has gone after the high end of the market in both Ho Chi Minh City and Hanoi. With the emerging population of office workers in these two cities, the company has been able to capitalize on the absence of a Starbucks in Vietnam. Highlands has gone after the lucrative "$3 cup of coffee" customer, while Trung Nguyen has marketed to the masses. Currently Highlands has 40 shops in Vietnam and the company has strategically placed itself in very high traffic and high-end office blocks in the downtown areas.[9]

LOCAL COMPETITION

In May 2006, AC Nielsen Vietnam conducted a survey among 3,000 people between 15 and 60 years old. The survey focused on brand name recognition across a broad range of industries and yielded some surprising results. Of the 500 famous brands that were highlighted, 50 percent of them were Vietnamese local brands with these brands dominating 3 out of 10 industries. Some of the best known brands included the following:

- Dong A Bank—financial services sector;
- Vinamilk—beverages;
- Viettel—telecommunications;
- Mai Linh Taxi—transportation;
- Dong Tam Tile—real estate and construction.

It's important to note that these are sizable companies with nationwide reach and popularity. Most are private with the exception of Viettel, which is a military-owned company, and most well known brands are from Ho Chi Minh City, which is the business hub of the country. So, Vietnam is not the virgin territory that it was a decade ago. There is sizable competition in almost any industry.[10] It's not possible to enter the country, assume it is a backwater, and dominate any industry no matter how much muscle and scale is being brought in.

It's important to understand how people compete in Vietnam. A story told by the executive director for business development and sales for a prominent multinational, who prefers to remain anonymous, illustrates a very important point.

"During my first national sales conference I came up with the idea of giving XYZ company dollars during the meeting. Anyone who participated and got an answer correct was given some play money. Nobody knew what the money was for but they knew they would somehow be rewarded.

On the last night we had a big dinner and I had organized about 25–30 prizes, which we planned to auction off using the company dollars. Well, nobody knew what an auction was so we ran through a couple of examples until everybody understood. I was the MC and put the first item up for bid and the fun started.

During the bidding for the first 20 prizes things went smoothly and everybody was having a blast. Then I saw all of the North Vietnamese sales people starting to congregate together. And I realized after they won the next bidding that they had pooled all of their money together. I did not think too much about it as we were almost done, but then I saw them flaunting the prize in front of the other sales teams and basically talking trash.

This went on for a couple more rounds before I saw the Central, South and Mekong teams get together to pool their money. Things escalated and before I knew it I had a mini war on my hands. They were arguing and screaming. It was complete pandemonium. The managers and I had to calm them down before we left. We organized some karaoke and after 30 minutes or so things were somewhat more relaxed and we went back to our hotel. They loved the auction and ask for it again every year but I finally stopped it because the northern teams always cheated or caused problems."

Situations like the one described above are rather common. There is a tendency towards chaos when large groups are brought together; it's noisy and boisterous. The facilitator or proctor is forgotten. It doesn't happen in formal seminar environments, but when any opportunity for interactivity is introduced, people get excited.

But more important to recognize is that the Vietnamese, like other Asian cultures, can be very collectivist when it suits their purpose. They aggregate around a common objective and are much more comfortable pursuing it as a group than as individuals.

They can also be fiercely competitive. Winning can be more important than the prize. It's a more pervasive and competitive norm than what is seen in westernized societies. Vietnamese also group together according to geography, as can be seen by the northern sales representatives grouping together against the South, Central and Mekong Delta teams. It can be assumed that in the face of competition from a foreign enterprise, the existing local competitors will band together in pursuit of a common strategy to ensure their survival. When doing a competitive analysis of any particular market in Vietnam, it may be best to view the local competitors as one entity rather than many. The seemingly fragmented businesses in a marketplace can rise up in unison when confronted by a common foreign competitor.

The tactics that companies can employ in Vietnam are also not as restricted as they are in the West. Collusion, price fixing and bribes paid in order to win contracts are all part of the competitive landscape in Vietnam. Intellectual property rights are harder to enforce. For example, the process to get a company's logo trademarked can take over a year. In many respects, the competition is more like the Wild West than a level and fair playing field. Copycats abound, as detailed elsewhere in the book, and protecting a company's image and product's integrity is a major challenge.

The U.S. Foreign Corrupt Practices Act prohibits American companies from engaging in bribes or other methods of non-transparent payment in order to secure a contract in competitive bid processes worldwide. European countries have guidelines governing their companies' behavior abroad in this respect as well. The situation in Vietnam is that non-transparent dealings often accompany contract bid processes. Corrupt government officials have been caught taking payments on government contracts. Local companies readily engage in graft on both sides of the contract. Companies that refuse to engage in these practices will be at a disadvantage in bidding on projects where the key decision maker is interested in lining his own pockets. The local competition is not bound by the same code of ethics as their Western counterparts.

The line between outright graft, bribes and corruption becomes blurred because of differences between cultures. The "red envelope" which has traditionally been given to children on holidays and to family members, employees and business partners on other important occasions has been extended to potential partners and clients with the size of the red envelope being fattened accordingly. In the mind of a Westerner this is a bribe. In the mind of the

Vietnamese, the distinction is much less clear. Whether this is just a convenient mutation of a tradition or a genuine cultural attribute doesn't matter all that much; the point is that not practicing puts one at a disadvantage in many situations.

A good example of this practice can be seen in the travel and leisure segment of the market, in particular hotels. Because Vietnam is a new and emerging destination in Asia, many companies have started to visit the country for meetings, conventions, and incentive trips for employees. When a travel agent books hotel rooms, excursions, meals and conference rooms are also booked which makes the potential value of the group booking much higher. It is not uncommon for the individual responsible for making bookings to have gifts of alcohol and gift baskets extended to them on important holidays. The gifts are extended to the individual, rather than the company. Go into any of the big travel agent offices during *Tet* and look across the desks of the booking agents piled high with personal "tokens" of appreciation. Exchanges of money are typically kept under the table. Gift giving has become an expectation of businesses and there can be little doubt as to whether it influences their decision-making.

Another example of the type of competition that can be expected from local companies in Vietnam is the recent case of JetStar Airlines. JetStar, an Australian-owned budget carrier, recently entered the Vietnam market through the acquisition of Pacific Airlines, which was a local carrier servicing domestic routes. The new airline became JetStar Pacific. The growing affluence of the country, a population of 85 million and the fact that there is only one other airline servicing the local routes (Vietnam Airlines) has made this particular market very attractive.

In a recent interview with an employee of Vietnam Airlines, the story of how JetStar's entry into the Vietnam market almost resulted in a costly failure was discussed. Being that Vietnam Airlines is the only domestic airline in the country, it makes sense that they also control Vietnam Air Petrol Company, the only company that supplies jet fuel to commercial airliners. Both companies are SOEs. Shortly after JetStar began operations in the domestic market in Vietnam in 2008, problems started to arise. At first, Vietnam Airlines decided to charge JetStar significantly more for its jet fuel than

Vietnam Airlines was paying. And then they decided that they just wouldn't supply the fuel at all.

For a country that has just joined the World Trade Organization, this type of anti-competitive behavior would be disastrous. Reportedly it took a phone call from a senior official at the People's Committee in Hanoi to the director of Vietnam Airlines to resolve the issue. JetStar is a large company making a sizable investment into Vietnam. This was enough to get the right people at the right level in the People's Committee involved to solve the issue. Smaller companies are subject to the same types of anti-competitive behavior, but will lack the importance to receive assistance if things get a little rough and dirty on the playing field of Vietnam business.

It should be noted that this story came from an employee of Vietnam Airlines, but that the information was not verifiable. JetStar Pacific would not discuss the issue either. There is always more to a story than meets the eye and this example should be taken with a grain of salt, and the understanding that the story surely goes deeper than the description given by one employee.

DISTRIBUTION

Vietnam follows a pretty standard Southeast Asian distribution model. Larger multinational firms prefer doing direct business and essentially try to reduce the role of the wholesalers. The market is fairly fragmented, so bigger companies can use their economies of scale, business knowledge and resources to offer better and more consistent service. However, many companies who rely on distribution note that the local wholesalers will offer more frequent deliveries and sometimes better pricing in order to move product. They seem willing to sacrifice the already small margins present in larger distribution-intensive industries like pharmaceuticals.

Many multinational firms run up against a "foreign company is evil" mentality. Over time however, buyers have come to understand that perception is different from reality and have gradually shown a propensity to buy based on what is best for them. Counterfeit products also show up much more in buying from the wholesalers as opposed to buying direct. Wholesalers, because of their more aggressive marketing strategies and reduced margins, gravitate towards poor product selection as a way to reduce costs.

Larger scale customers like hospitals or grocery store chains, although more lucrative business partners because of their size, are less transparent in their business dealings. The decision makers in this space may be interested in kickbacks or other forms of personal incentives to get business. Effort spent in pursuing this business is not wasted though. One distribution manager for a larger packaged foods producer notes that many wholesalers simply cannot manage the demand of a very big client. The volumes are too large and the outstanding balances put a strain on their resources.

Other countries in Asia can be even more fragmented than Vietnam. Nonetheless, size is important in any business that is going to require large-scale distribution to be successful. Without the proper scale, wholesalers are needed which puts a company at a disadvantage to any competitor that is selling directly. Bigger multinational companies have an advantage. Dutch Lady, Unilever, Procter and Gamble and Nestlé are just some of the massive multinationals that have been in Vietnam for many years now and dominate their respective industries.

Legally, foreign enterprises do not have full trading and distribution rights in Vietnam, although licenses have been granted on a case-by-case basis. Alternatively, a partnership with a local company must be set up to facilitate distribution. The bilateral trade agreement signed with the United States in 2001 was the first step in opening up the retail space to foreign companies, and entry into the WTO has further moved things along. Phase-in periods are in place, so the move to a totally free marketplace will certainly not happen overnight.

MANAGING A LOCAL SALES FORCE

Managing a sales team in Vietnam is critical to any business that intends to sell into the local market. Some of the dynamics are illustrated in the following interview with a sales executive who's worked for many years with a global distributor of pharmaceuticals, but who prefers to remain anonymous.

BV: What was your biggest challenge in managing a sales force in Vietnam?

AN: Well, I had a very large sales team covering the entire country. The problem is that a sales representative is not really a respected profession in Vietnam. Teachers are respected, which is different from what is often seen in Western cultures. The sales reps did not have a lot of confidence and were submissive in front of customers. A Western sales rep will take control of an account and really lead them to where the SR wants to go. The average sales rep here is fairly lazy and does not see the big picture, so any new initiative was not welcomed because it represents more work.

BV: Interesting. I've always heard that the Vietnamese are extremely hard workers.

AN: One of my biggest disappointments was that when I arrived in Vietnam I thought the Vietnamese would have a much better work ethic than the Thais. I came from our Thailand office to Vietnam. I do not think this was true for the average SR. However, I had some managers and staff that worked extremely hard.

BV: What did you do to motivate them and address this problem?

AN: In 2005, I organized a third party SR audit. The SRs were trained on what they should do during a call and provided with new sales tools to help them. The third party observed and recorded the conversation between the SR and the customer. Part of an SR's incentives was based on his performance. This really motivated the SRs to improve, and we also started an SR of the year and a SR promotion program, which rewarded the best SRs. Vietnamese are competitive so these programs work well to promote change and to identify the stars.

BV: Building on this, what skills do you think need to be focused on in order to establish a successful sales team? What skills are most lacking?

AN: Where do I start? Long-term thinking is not a focus yet, whether it is brand-building or customer service. The idea of a win-win is not common, so they end up screwing people to make a sale. They tend to think of things in terms of commodities. This means they really do not understand branding, value and strategy. They are more interested in moving product from one level of distribution and making a small percentage.

BV: So a foreign sales manager coming into Vietnam, to manage a local team, is going to need which skills in order to succeed?

AN: Vietnam requires a lot of micromanaging. Every day there is a new problem that has to be resolved. It is easy to forget about strategy because managers are sometimes just trying to keep the organization running. So focus is important. Flexibility is a must, but still staying true to the long-term agenda. A sense of humor is helpful when things go wrong. Patience and a willingness to speak in broken English until you receive the whole story and not only the part they want to tell you. Sometimes this is exhausting. I think real type A personalities struggle in Vietnam. And finally, a recognition that the north and south are different and have to be managed differently. Actually, in my experience, the northern sales reps that I had to manage were much more difficult than the south.

BV: Sounds like a lot to worry about. What positive things does a foreign sales manager have going for him?

AN: I think the Vietnamese that I managed enjoyed a participative/ foreign management style. We tend to engage the people and build good relationships by taking care of the people. They are not used to somebody showing an interest in them and their development. They also like to brag that their boss is a foreigner. And of course there is a strong desire to work for a foreign company because there is the perception, and in most cases the reality, that they pay better.

A lot can be taken from these insights and applied to sales teams in Vietnam. The average sales rep is fairly representative of the average worker. What's more important to glean from this interview is that things will be different here. The history of the country is too dynamic and unique to allow for the extrapolation of an experience elsewhere to work here. That said, many of the same things that motivate and incentivize people in the West also work well in Vietnam. Other things don't. And even within the country, different strategies may need to be employed to get the most out of, say, a Hanoi-based team versus one based in Ho Chi Minh City.

One unique attribute of the labor force in Vietnam, that makes managing them difficult, is the short-term focus that is mentioned in the interview. Sales people aren't interested in developing long-term relationships that generate sales in the future. They are interested in manipulating a situation to make a sale now with no regard for future impact. This may be a result of the subsistence level in the country until very recently, or possibly the war. Regardless of the cause, it exists and can be damaging to a company if not realized and dealt with.

ADVERTISING

Advertising has been permitted in Vietnam only since 1990, and the industry is heavily regulated. Only companies that are licensed to do business in Vietnam may place advertisements. Alcohol and tobacco cannot be marketed in the mass media. Many sectors require registration and approvals before advertising content can be run, and the Ministry of Culture and Information oversees and approves all content. Despite this control and regulation, there are about 20 international advertising agencies in Vietnam. The presence of these agencies in Vietnam is mostly for the sake of catering to multinational firms with global accounts.

In 2004, television made up 53.5 percent, print media 24.5 percent and outdoor advertising 21 percent of the total advertising mix.[11] One important sector that is not measured in these statistics is online advertising. The access and exposure rate to the internet is very high in Vietnam. Anyone who does not have a computer can easily gain access to one through the numerous internet cafes that can be found in even the smallest towns. Yahoo! and other online advertising giants have resources that are specifically concentrated on the country now. Local companies have their own websites; Vietnam's rate of internet use is similar to that in developed countries.

Marketing media pursued by businesses in advertising their products has exploded in Vietnam with the growth of the private business sector. The country has made huge strides from the days of government marketing in the form of propaganda signs on the sides of the roads. There are still smatterings of propaganda signs, but they are more pursued as "art" rather than advertising outlets. Tourists hunt them down in antique shops in the old quarter of Hanoi to hang on their walls as historical relics when they return home.

There are a number of English language newspapers in Vietnam that have advertising space for sale. The country has about 400 newspapers and other printed publications. These media serve as good outlets for advertising given the high literacy rate. *Vietnam News* is probably the most mainstream and widely distributed of the English language papers. It is read by many of the expatriate population in the country and small advertisements can be taken out just as they would in the West. *Saigon Times* is another widely distributed paper. It tends to be more "businessy" but also offers advertising space.

The Vietnamese language newspapers are widely read. Book availability was very limited for a long time, so the habit and practice of reading a newspaper is the primary means of getting information. There is a wider range and availability of newspapers and people tend to be focused on local news, which affects them directly. This is changing slowly as the country opens up, people travel more, and an interest in the world outside of Vietnam intensifies.

The penetration rate of television into people's homes has made pursuing advertisements through this media much more enticing and potentially lucrative. Ninety-two percent of the 18 million of Vietnam's urban population own televisions (92 percent in Ho Chi Minh City and 96 percent in Hanoi). International stations such as CNN and StarTV are easily accessible because of the emergence of satellite dishes. Television advertising rates have jumped over the years with a 500 percent increase seen from 1994 to 1999, and the purchasing of airtime is highly concentrated among a few very large companies.[12]

Vietnam has not escaped the flat screen liquid crystal display craze. The technology is very popular. Sony Vietnam recently announced the closure of its $16.5 million factory near Ho Chi Minh City, which produces picture tube televisions, because of the switch worldwide (including Vietnam) to flat screens.[13] The Vietnamese put a large percentage of their newfound wealth into modern appliances.

Other advertising media that could be considered in Vietnam include out-door billboards, signboards, and radio. Radio offers a cost-effective alternative over television, and billboards are used by many companies seeking to build brand awareness in the country. Be cautious of signboard space that is for rent, as many of these outdoor spaces are illegal.

Finally, as noted elsewhere in this book, the Vietnamese have not been marketed to as heavily as Western populations have. They are more receptive to it and less put off by obvious attempts to get them to buy something. A strong culture of consumerism is building in the country, mostly in response to a rush of previously unavailable products. Less sophisticated marketing and advertising approaches are likely to work well.

PIRATED PRODUCTS AND COPIES: HOW THEY ARE VIEWED

Pirated and copied products still dominate the marketplace in Vietnam. They can be found everywhere in the country in products ranging from footwear, apparel, and DVDs to cosmetics and cell phones. Some of the fakes are so good that it is very difficult to recognize them. Many products that you find in the marketplace *are* real, but sell at much reduced prices from normal retail outlets. The reason for this is that there are a large number of companies manufacturing in Vietnam, and control at the factories is often lax. A factory that is producing shoes for Merrell during the day may be kept open at night in order to run more shoes off the line and sell directly into the local market. Tourists can be seen shopping at the outdoor kiosks and finding great deals on products. The Vietnamese have moved into this "in between" market where real products can be obtained at unreal (bargain) prices.

The Vietnamese aren't big fans of knock-offs, copies and fakes, but they buy these products because of their income limitations. If they have the money to buy an original item, they will. They are quality conscious when it comes to consumer products. The consumer hierarchy goes something like this:

1. Those who buy fakes because that's what they can afford.
2. Those who purchase real products that are over-runs and sold in outdoor kiosks.
3. Those who are as concerned about being seen as they are about buying genuine products at full retail prices. These consumers tend to be young and wealthy.

It can be assumed that as the population grows more affluent, copies and fakes will become less popular.

SUMMARY

Vietnam's market is immature. This presents both extreme opportunities and daunting challenges. There are a fantastic number of success stories. Both large multinationals and smaller local companies have succeeded in the Vietnam market. The market is eager for new products and growing in affluence.

There are an even greater number of failed business examples. Companies have entered the country and misread the marketplace, underestimated the competition and overestimated the workforce. Vietnam is unique. It has a checkered recent history that makes it different from its neighboring countries in Southeast Asia. It should be assumed that the same model that has worked elsewhere will not work in Vietnam. The country has to be studied and the marketplace understood before any measure of success can be expected.

ENDNOTES

1. "Vietnam at a Glance," World Bank, September 28, 2007, http://devdata .worldbank.org/AAG/vnm_aag.pdf
2. "Vietnam Mobile Phone Market Hots Up," Apec Digital Opportunity Center, May 11, 2008, http://www.apecdoc.org/node/6770
3. Ibid.
4. "Let the Good Times Roll," *Vietnam Investment Review*, March 28, 2005, http:// www.vir.com.vn/client/VIR/index.asp?url=content.asp&doc=6676
5. Ibid.
6. Ibid.
7. Trung Nguyen coffee, http://www.trungnguyen.com.vn/en/default.aspx?c=156# content
8. "Vietnam's Trung Nguyen Coffee Opens Franchise in Singapore," Yahoo! Asia News, September 12, 2008, http://asia.news.yahoo.com/080912/4/3oxhq.html
9. Highlands Coffee, http://www.highlandscoffee.com.vn/aboutus_whoweare.html
10. "Best Known Brands in Vietnam Recognized," CACCI Profile, May 2006, www.cacci.org.tw/CACCI%20Profile/2006/May/VCCI%20best.pdf
11. *Business Law Handbook 2008*, 4th Edition, Global Investment Center, Washington, D.C.
12. Ibid.
13. "Sony to Stop Manufacturing Televisions in Vietnam in September," July 25, 2008, Monsters and Critics Business News, http://www.monstersandcritics. com/news/business/news/article_1419316.php/Sony_to_stop_manufacturing_ televisions_in_Vietnam_in_September

CHAPTER 10

Intellectual Property Rights

IPR CHALLENGES AND REALITIES IN VIETNAM

When someone creates an original work, idea or process, there are certain monopoly rights that are often granted in order to foster such innovation. These creations are referred to as intellectual property. Oftentimes, intellectual property is defined as four separate types of intangible assets: patents, copyrights, trademarks and trade secrets.

Many Vietnamese struggle to see the value of intellectual property protection. Some argue that artists such as Madonna and record labels like Warner Brothers are wealthy enough, so what is the harm in copying and selling their work without giving them a cut? For people who battle poverty on a daily basis, selling fake CDs may mean the vendor and his family can eat a good dinner that night when they otherwise couldn't. It also means that their customers can enjoy movies, music and other internationally created content that they couldn't afford otherwise.

Some Vietnamese on the other hand realize that companies or persons will not bring innovative new products, processes and other ideas into a country that doesn't offer them some level of protection. The challenge is to convince the Vietnamese that intellectual property protection will offer more benefits to them in the long run.

Hong van Phuong, Science and Technology Minister, was quoted by Vietnam News as saying:

"The courts should play a more important role in dealing with IPR violations. Currently however, we only have administrative measures to deal with such violations. If a person violates intellectual property rights, the case uses an arbitrator. Under IPR laws, together with administrative measures, violators must compensate the copyright or patent owner and consumers, but penalties still fall short.

Vietnam is considering whether to treat such violations as criminal cases. Whether a case is civil or criminal will be determined by the courts. In industrial countries, the courts' role in IPR is considered important, yet this is still new to Vietnam.

One problem is that the courts lack experience in and understanding of intellectual property rights, so as a result they have not established separate legal proceedings to handle IPR as in other countries.

Only the courts can offer a definitive solution; administrative measures can only stop violations; they will not solve the overall problem.

In the future, serious violations need the courts' attention. The courts must take an active part in cases soon, so we can integrate successfully into the international market."

The following well-known case illustrates the problems that international firms are experiencing in Vietnam.

Copied Contraceptives Pulled from Market

Ho Chi Minh City—"The contraceptive pill Posinight 2 will be withdrawn from the Vietnamese market," said an official from the Pharmaceuticals Management Department under the Health Ministry.

The announcement was made after the department found that Posinight 2, manufactured by Binh Duong Pharmaceuticals and Medical Equipment Company, was a complete imitation, from the packaging to the pills inside of the imported morning-after pill, Postinor 2.

Hungarian pharmaceutical company Gedeon Richter, the producer of Postinor 2, filed a lawsuit against the Binh Duong Pharmaceuticals and Medical Equipment Co in early November after presenting the situation to the Pharmaceutical Management Department and the Ministry of Science and Technology's intellectual property department.

Some 400 fake and imitation goods have been seized by police between 2000 and 2004, according to figures released at a seminar on fighting fake and imitation goods in Ha Noi in October.[1]

The Gedeon Richter (GR) vs. Binh Duong Pharmaceuticals and Medical Equipment Company (BIPHARCO) case was the first court case in Ho Chi Minh City based on unfair competition relating to pharmaceutical intellectual property rights. The court awarded GR approximately $46,000 in damages, although GR was unhappy with the amount as they claimed that their actual losses were in excess of this figure.[2]

Unfortunately for GR, the case later went to appeal, where the court upheld the unfair competition finding but found that GR had failed to prove actual damages suffered as a result of BIPHARCO's infringement. Because the court ruled that GR didn't sufficiently prove their actual loss from BIPHARCO's infringement, the court withdrew the award of damages.[3]

During an Intellectual Property Rights (IPR) roundtable hosted by the former U.S. Ambassador to Vietnam, Michael Marine, four primary challenges associated with protecting IPR in Vietnam were highlighted:[4]

1. Legal deficiencies: Penalties are comparatively lenient when compared with those imposed by most industrialized countries. Definitions are inadequate and coverage is spotty, relative to international IPR treaties.

2. Poor enforcement:
   - Judicial remedies are limited due to weak court systems and inadequately trained judges.
   - Several government bodies are involved, and they lack strong coordination.
3. The public is unaware of the importance of IPR protection.
4. The country lacks strong property right holders' associations.

Unfortunately, Vietnam has one of the highest pirating and counterfeiting rates in the world. According to the Business Software Alliance (BSA), the percentage of computers in Vietnam with pirated software loaded on them dropped from 92 percent in 2003 to 85 percent in 2007. While this is a move in the right direction for software companies, the overall piracy rate is still much higher than in Asia Pacific's best practice countries such as Singapore, which had a 37 percent piracy rate in 2007. The estimated losses for the software industry in Vietnam currently stand in the $200 million range.[5]

In an interview with *Vietnam News*, Nguyen Manh Hung, Deputy Director of the Market Watch Department, had this to say:

"Over the past few years, the fight by ministries, departments and agencies against counterfeit goods, commonly referred to as IPR violations, has made some progress.

Last year, there were 2,256 cases of various types of IPR violations in the country.

Producing and selling of counterfeit goods has not been significantly reduced given progress is very difficult and complicated. Fake goods are not only a concern for companies and consumers, but they also damage the economy and corporate confidence and put public health and the environment at risk.

According to the prime minister's Decree 31, fighting counterfeit goods is a social responsibility. Relevant agencies and authorities at all levels, including social and professional associations, the Vietnam Lawyers Association, and consumer rights organizations all play an

important role in exposing IPR violations and fighting against the production and trade of counterfeit goods.

Market watch teams are addressing the fight with several projects.
We have begun training courses for staff to boost awareness and legal
understanding of IPR issues; co-operated with international organizations in educating businesses about IPR laws; and organized exhibitions
on how to differentiate between counterfeit and real goods in central
and provincial areas so agencies, companies and especially the public
can identify the differences."[6]

THE PATH TO PROTECTION

Given these challenges, how can you protect your intellectual property
in Vietnam? While it isn't always easy, there are some measures that you
can take.

Patents

Vietnamese law regarding patents originates in the 1995 Civil Code. In Vietnam, the process for firming up legislation is to pass a law and follow up
with one or several decrees and circulars, which serve to clarify the law and
how it should be implemented. In the case of patents, Decree 63 guides the
implementation of the Civil Code, whereas Circular 34 of the Ministry of
Science and Technology (MOST) provides for the creation of patent rights.
The length of the patent life varies depending on the type of patent. For
example, patents for utility solutions are valid for 10 years, while patents
for industrial designs have a shorter five-year lifespan. Unfortunately for the
design holder of patents for inventions and utility solutions, these types of
patents are non-renewable. However, holders of patents for industrial designs
can renew the patent for up to two successive five-year periods. Table 10.1
illustrates the number of patents granted in Vietnam from 1990 to 2005.

Table 10.1   Granted patents for inventions, 1990–2005

Year	Vietnamese Applicants	Foreign Applicants	Total
1990	11	3	14
1991	14	13	27
1992	19	16	35
1993	3	13	16
1994	5	14	19
1995	3	53	56
1996	4	58	62
1997	0	111	111
1998	5	343	348
1999	13	322	335
2000	10	620	630
2001	7	776	783
2002	9	734	743
2003	17	757	774
2004	22	676	698
2005	27	641	668

Source: National Office of Intellectual Property, Vietnam, 2005
Annual Report

1,947 applications for patents of inventions were sought, of which 91 percent were granted to non-Vietnamese entities. In contrast, the U.S. granted 157,717 patents in 2005, of which 48 percent were of foreign origin.[7]

In addition to the coverage of utility and industrial designs, the IP Law provides for protection of layout-designs of semiconductor integrated circuits until the end of 10 years from the filing date or from the date the layout-designs were commercially exploited anywhere in the world by the licensee, and 15 years from the creation date of the layout-designs.

When you have inventions, industrial designs, layout-designs (integrated circuits) or utility solutions that you'd like to protect in Vietnam, you should go immediately to the Ministry of Science and Technology because Vietnam's patent registration system functions on a first-to-file basis. Priority is based on either the date on which the National Office of Industrial Property (NOIP) receives the application or the date on which it was postmarked, and priority is also given to previously registered patents in other countries pursuant to treaty obligations.

Unfortunately, there are many processes that cannot be registered, including: computer software; prevention, diagnostic and/or therapeutic methods for treatment of humans and animals; discoveries, scientific theories and/or mathematical methods, schemes, plans, rules or methods for performing mental acts; training domestic animals; playing games; doing business; presentations of information; solutions of aesthetic characteristics only; plant or animal varieties; and processes of essentially biological nature for the production of plants and animals other than microbiological processes.

For items that can be registered, the patent owner holds exclusive rights to the patent during its lifetime. Patents can be registered with the Ministry of Science and Technology's National Office of Intellectual Property. The law provides various remedies for infringement. Use of the patented item without prior consent by the patent owner is considered infringement.

Under the law, patent owners can enforce their rights in four ways:

- Request that the state agencies handle acts of infringement of intellectual property rights in accordance with provisions of the law and other related laws and regulations;
- Take measures such as using technology to prevent violation of their intellectual property rights;
- Request that people or groups that have committed acts of infringement terminate the infringing acts and apologize, and/or publicly rectify and compensate damages; and/or
- Sue to protect legitimate rights and interests.

Copyrights

Part Six of Vietnam's 1995 Civil Code included the country's first provisions on copyrights. Since then, Vietnam has continued to introduce legislation to ensure that international standards under Trade-Related aspects of International Property Rights (TRIPS) and the Berne Convention are being met. Decree 76/CP, published in 1996, provides explicit guidance on the implementation of copyright protection. Criminal penalties for copyright in-fringement were established under Section 131 of the 1999 Criminal Code. Circular 27/2001/TT-BVHTT of May 10, 2001 provided additional guidance to the Ministry of Culture and Information on implementation of copyright protection. The newly enacted Civil Code of 2005 reiterates Vietnam's com-mitment to protect copyrights. Specific details of copyright protection, such as content, scope, time limits of protection and transferability of IP rights, are addressed in the Law on Intellectual Property.

In contrast to trademarks and patents, copyrights are granted once the copyrightable work is created, and copyrights that are granted within treaty countries are immediately applicable to all other treaty countries. However, persons may still voluntarily apply for a copyright certificate in Vietnam. Detailed application instructions and application materials may be found at the Copyright Office within the Ministry of Culture and Information.

Copyrightable material includes literary and scientific works; textbooks; teaching materials and other works expressed in forms of letters or other writing characters (such as Chinese characters); lectures; presentations and other speeches; journalistic, musical, or dramatic works; cinematographic works and works created by similar methods; works of fine art, photography, and architecture; computer programs and compilations of data can also be copyrighted as can graphics, sketches, maps, drawings relevant to topography and scientific works.

Copyright infringement entails using, reproducing, reprinting, importing, exporting, selling, publishing, disseminating, or otherwise exploiting a copy-righted work without prior written permission from the author or the copy-right owner and/or without appropriate remuneration through royalties or other financial duties to either the author or legal owner of the copyright.

Where to Apply for a Copyright Certificate

Ministry of Culture and Information
Copyright Office
151 Hoang Hoa Tham
Hanoi, Vietnam

Phone: (84-4) 823-6908
Fax: (84-4) 843-2630

Representative Office in Ho Chi Minh City
7 Nguyen Thi Minh Khai, Q. 1
Ho Chi Minh City, Vietnam
Phone: (84-8) 823-4132
Fax: (84-8) 823-4940

Trade Secrets

Trade secrets are also accorded protection in the IP Law. They are officially referred to in Chapter VII, Section 7 as "business secrets." The law provides for the protection of trade secrets from unlawful use, but at the time of this writing there was no actual registration process in place. Violation of trade secrets entails knowingly disclosing or using the trade secret without prior permission from the secret's owner or breaking a contract with the owner over the agreed concealment of the secret.

Trademarks

As with copyrights, protection of trademarks was first addressed in the Civil Code of 1995. Subsequently, Vietnam joined the Madrid System for International Registration of Marks. Since then, many decrees and circulars have given further clarification to the implementation of trademark registration and protection. The most recent Law on Intellectual Property specifies with greater detail the criteria for determining well-known marks, such as a company's logo, as well as criteria for legal protections. The NOIP reports that it received some 18,000 trademark applications in 2005, reflecting a 17 percent rise compared to the previous year. The laws and regulations apply to service and collective marks and trade names. Service marks operate much like trade names, but are used to identify a particular service, rather than a product. Collective marks, on the other hand, are oftentimes used by associations whose members use the collective mark to identify themselves with a high level of quality, or another characteristic set by the association. A sign in the form of pictures, letters, words, and figures, including three-dimensional figures or a combination of these, in one or more colors and distinguishing the offerings of the mark owner from those of others, can be registered as a trademark.

As with patents, trademarks are awarded on a first-to-file basis and priority provisions are given as well. The NOIP has three months to review and verify the application for completeness. Once it is deemed complete, NOIP takes approximately nine months to evaluate the merit of a request. If approved, trademark registrations have a ten-year lifespan. Information on associated fees and paperwork can be accessed from the NOIP. In addition to trademarks, service marks and collective marks, for the first time the IP Law also provides protection for trade names in Vietnam.

The following items cannot be trademarked: signs identical with or very similar to the national flags and emblems; armorial bearings; abbreviations; full names of state agencies; political, socio-political and socio-political professional organizations; social or socio-professional organizations of Vietnam or international organizations, unless permitted by such agencies or organizations; real, alias and pen names or images of leaders; national heroes or famous persons of Vietnam or foreign countries; signs identical with or confusingly similar to certification seals; control seals; warranty seals of international organizations which require that their signs must not be used, except where such seals are registered as certification marks by those organizations; signs liable to mislead, confuse or deceive consumers as to the origin, functional parameters, intended purposes, quality, value or other characteristics of the goods or services.

Informal and private mediation of trademark disputes is usually considered to be more effective than formal judicial and administrative methods. However, the law does provide for various civil, criminal and administrative punishments. The administrative agencies have broad powers in sanctioning trademark infringement, which includes the power to seize and destroy counterfeit materials and to issue cease-and-desist orders, revoke licenses and impose fines.

Where to file for Patents and Register Trademarks:

Ministry of Science and Technology
National Office of Intellectual Property (NOIP)
386 Nguyen Trai Street
Thanh Xuan
Hanoi
Phone: (84-4) 858-3069/858-3425/858-3973
Fax: (84-4) 858-4002/858-8449

Intellectual Property Rights Resources

- An excellent guide to protecting intellectual property, the IPR Toolkit for Vietnam, is available from the U.S. Commercial Service (see http://www.buyusa.gov/vietnam/en/ipr_toolkit.html).
- Agreement on Trade-Related Aspects of Intellectual Property; http://www.wto.org/english/tratop_e/trips_e/trips_e.htm
- ASEAN Framework Agreement on Intellectual Property; Cooperation; http://www.aseansec.org/2193.htm
- Berne Convention for the Protection of Literary and Artistic Works; http://www.wipo.int/treaties/en/ip/berne/index.html
- Bilateral Intellectual Property Agreement between Vietnam and Switzerland (1999); http://www.cov.org.vn/English/viewNew.asp?newId=41
- Bilateral Trade Agreement between Vietnam and the United States of America (2000); http://hanoi.usembassy.gov/econ12.html
- Biotechnology Industry Organization; http://www.bio.org/
- Business Software Alliance (BSA); http://www.bsa.org/
- Civil Code, Part Six (2005); http://www.cov.org.vn/English/viewNew.asp?newId=135
- Convention for the Protection of Producers of Phonograms against Unauthorized Duplication of their Phonograms; http://www.wipo.int/treaties/en/ip/phonograms/index.html
- Entertainment Software Association; http://www.theesa.com/

- IIPA - International Intellectual Property Alliance; http://www.iipa.com
- International Anti-Counterfeiting Coalition; http://www.iacc.org/
- International Federation of the Phonographic Industry (IFPI); http://www.ifpi.org/
- International Research-Based Pharmaceutical Manufacturers Association (IRPMA); http://www.irpma.org.tw/english
- International Trademark Association; http://www.inta.org/
- Law on Intellectual Property (2006); http://www.noip.gov.vn/noip/cms_en.nsf
- Madrid Agreement Concerning the International Registration of Marks; http://www.wipo.int/treaties/en/ip/madrid/index.html
- Ministry of Culture and Information Copyright Office; http://www.cov.org.vn
- Ministry of Finance General Department of Vietnam Customs; http://www.customs.gov.vn/Default.aspx?tabid=762
- Ministry of Science, Technology and Environment National Office of Intellectual Property; http://www.noip.gov.vn
- Motion Picture Association; http://www.mpaa.org/
- Music Publishers Association; http://www.mpa.org/
- Paris Convention for the Protection of Industrial Property: http://www.wipo.int/treaties/en/ip/paris/index.html
- Rome Convention for the Protection of Performers, Producers of Phonograms and Broadcasting Organizations; http://www.wipo.int/treaties/en/ip/rome/index.html
- World Intellectual Property Organization (WIPO); http://www.wipo.int
- World Trade Organization, TRIPS; http://www.wto.org/english/tratop_e/trips_e/trips_e.htm

Legal Counsel and IPR Advice in Vietnam

- Ageless IP Attorneys and Consultants; http://www.ageless.com.vn/
- Anphamco Co. Ltd.; http://anphamco.com/
- Baker & McKenzie; http://www.bakernet.com

- Bizconsult Attorneys and Consultants; http://www.bizconsult-vietnam. com/public/index.htm
- D&N Intellectual Property Law Firm; http://www.dnlaw.com.vn/Home/ main.php
- Gia Pham Law Firm; http://www.law.com.vn/
- Gintasset Intellectual Property Law Firm; http://www.gintasset.com.vn/
- Investconsults Group; http://www.investconsultgroup.net
- InvestPro and Associates; http://www.investpro.com.vn/
- IP Menu; http://www.ipmenu.com/ipfirms/vietnam.htm
- Rouse & Co. International; http://www.iprights.com/
- Tilleke & Gibbins; http://www.tillekeandgibbins.com/Office/localmap_ HoChiMinh.htm

ENDNOTES

1. "Copied Contraceptives Pulled from Market," *Vietnam News*, January 10, 2005, http://vietnamnews.vnagency.com.vn/showarticle.php?num=02ECO100105
2. "Law News: Competition is not Healthy: 2 Pharmaceutical Enterprises Penalty USD46,000," [trans], January 4, 2006, http://translate.google.com/translate? hl=en&sl=vi&u=http://www.vntrades.com/tintuc/name-News-file-article-sid-4742.htm&sa=X&oi=translate&resnum=6&ct=result&prev=/search%3Fq% 3DPOSTINOR2%2BPOSINIGHT2%26hl%3Den%26rls%3Dcom.microsoft:en-US%26rlz%3D1I7GGIE_en%26sa%3DN
3. "Intellectual Property Rights Primer," Version V.1.1, https://www.uktradeinvest. gov.uk/ukti/fileDownload/IPR_Vietnam.pdf?cid=422403
4. Presentation from USAID Funded STAR-VIETNAM Project to U.S. Ambassador's Roundtable on IPR, April 28, 2005, http://www.usvtc.org/trade/ipr/STAR _IPR_28apr05.pdf
5. Business Software Alliance's 2007 Global Software Piracy Study, May 2008, http://global.bsa.org/idcglobalstudy2007//studies/summaryfindings_ globalstudy07.pdf
6. "Courts, Public Central to Battling Intellectual Property Violations," April 5, 2007, *Vietnam Economic Times*, http://vietnamnews.vnagency.com.vn/ showarticle.php?num=01COM050407
7. U.S. Patent Statistics Chart, Calendar Years 1963 - 2007, U.S. Patent and Trade-mark Office, http://www.uspto.gov/go/taf/us_stat.htm

CHAPTER 11

Tax

Taxes are important to any country. Without tax revenue, there would be no money for the infrastructure projects, public goods, and services that are essential for any properly functioning society. From a business standpoint, what we get for the taxes we pay matters a great deal. For example, if there are high taxes, and the quality of the infrastructure is poor, our company suffers. When we conduct business in lower-tax jurisdictions with high quality infrastructures (all else being equal) our company thrives.

Efficient tax authorities tend to have less complex tax systems, with clear compliance procedures and straightforward laws. According to the World Bank, there is a high correlation between less complex tax systems and benefits to taxpayers. Burdensome tax systems often trigger tax evasion.

Vietnam's tax regime is complex and burdensome. Preferential tax arrangements are sometimes offered at the central, provisional, municipal, or the industrial-zone level, with the tax authorities having considerable discretion to grant such incentives on a case-by-case basis. However, with Vietnam's accession into the World Trade Organization (WTO), the country is in the process of ending performance-related incentives tied to exports.

TAXATION OVERVIEW

In recognition of the complexities of the pre-existing tax system, Vietnam implemented a law on tax administration in 2007. The law governs both corporate and personal taxation and extends a system of self-declaration and self-payment of tax.[1] In addition to this law update, there is a new law on personal income tax that was issued in November 2007, which was implemented as of

January 1, 2009. The major components of the personal income tax update include: additional rules regarding tax residency, a broadening of the tax base, removal of tax treatment concessions of some benefit items, personal and family deduction changes, unified tax rates applicable to both Vietnamese and foreigners, and increased compliance obligations. Also as of January 2009, the normal corporate income tax rate was cut from 28 percent to 25 percent, and value-added tax (VAT) changes are expected to be updated. The details of the new corporate income tax and VAT regimes remain largely unknown because, at the time of writing, there are no implementing circulars giving pertinent details for either the law on corporate income tax or the law on VAT. Thus, the details of changes to the corporate tax rate and much of the information about the VAT included here are valid up to and including December 31, 2008.

We strongly suggest that you use this chapter as a starting point for your understanding of the tax system with the knowledge that the tax system is receiving a major overhaul. There is no guarantee that the information provided here is still valid at the time that you are reading it, or that it will be valid in the future.

For other Asian tax systems such as Hong Kong or Singapore, it is possible to meet your tax obligations easily. With online filing and one-page tax returns in English, those systems cater to foreign interests. In Vietnam, however, it is imperative that your company and personal tax situations be reviewed by an expert, *especially* if you are not a fluent Vietnamese speaker. A list of reputable contacts can be found at the end of this chapter.

BUSINESS TAXATION

According to the World Bank, Vietnam's business tax processes are more burdensome than those found in other Southeast Asian countries including Malaysia, Thailand, Laos, Indonesia, and even the Philippines. In fact, of 181 countries surveyed, Vietnam was ranked 140th of 181 in terms of ease and costs of making business tax payments.

In order to unify the different tax systems for Vietnamese entities and foreign investment enterprises, corporate tax rates and regulations were revised substantially from 2004. Foreign investment enterprises licensed since January 1, 2004, are subject to the current laws, but foreign investment enterprises licensed before this date are still subject to the tax rates stipulated in their licenses. Official Letter 10997 of the Ministry of Finance (MoF) abolished the preferential corporate income tax policy for newly listed firms on the Vietnamese stock exchanges as from January 1, 2007.

Most foreign businesses will be affected by the following taxes in Vietnam:

- Business income tax;
- Capital assignment profits tax;
- Import duties;
- Personal income tax of Vietnamese and expatriate employees;
- Social security and health insurance premiums for Vietnamese employees;
- Value added tax;
- Various withholding taxes.

Other taxes that may affect certain investors include:

- Export duties;
- Natural resources tax;
- Property taxes;
- Special sales tax.

All of the above mentioned taxes are imposed at the national level. There are no additional local, state or provincial taxes.

The standard corporate income tax rate is 25 percent; preferential rates apply when certain conditions are satisfied. Article 13 of the Law on Enterprise Income Tax, which became effective on January 1, 2009, outlines the following tax incentives:

1. Newly set up enterprises under investment projects in geographical areas with extreme socio-economic difficulties, economic zones or hi-tech parks; newly set up enterprises under investment projects in the domains

of high technology, scientific research and technological development, development of the State's infrastructure, works of special importance, or manufacture of software products are entitled to the tax rate of 10 percent for 15 years.

2. Enterprises operating in education-training, vocational training, healthcare, cultural, sports and environmental domains are entitled to the tax rate of 10 percent.

3. Newly set up enterprises under investment projects in geographical areas with socio-economic difficulties are entitled to the tax rate of 20 percent for 10 years.

4. Agricultural service cooperatives and people's credit funds are entitled to the tax rate of 20 percent.

5. For large-scale and hi-tech projects in which investment should be particularly attracted, the duration for application of tax rate incentives may be extended but must not exceed the duration specified in Clause 1 of this Article.

6. The duration for application of tax rate incentives specified in this Article is counted from the first year an enterprise shows income.

(The Government shall detail and guide the implementation of this Article.)[2]

Calculating Business Taxable Income

Taxable profits are defined as the difference between total revenue, regardless of whether the revenue is sourced domestically or internationally, and total deductible expenses, plus other profits of the company in the tax year, minus losses that may be carried forward to the following year. Profit also covers that of any affiliates and branches.

Revenue includes:

• Provision of services;
• Sales of products;
• Any other income.

Income subject to taxation includes income from:

- Joint-venture operations with other economic entities;
- Leasing or sale of assets;
- Transfer of shares.

Foreign investors with a range of business-co-operation contracts (BCCs) must account for each separately.

Certain types of interest income earned by foreign investors are taxable and subject to tax withheld at the source of the income. Banks are required to withhold corporate income tax from interest payments made to foreign investors.

Taxpayers are required to prepare an annual corporate income tax return, which includes a section for making adjustments between accounting profits and taxable income.

Deductions

Tax deductions are allowed for reasonable expenses. For example, the following expenditures are considered deductible:

- Acquisition costs or fees paid for the right to use technical documents, patents, technology and technical services;
- Advertising and promotion expenses up to a maximum of 10 percent of all deductible expenses;
- Costs of insuring assets of the enterprise (provided the insurer is licensed to operate in Vietnam);
- Costs of raw materials and fuel to manufacture principal products and by-products or to provide services;
- Costs of termination of employment (up to one month of salary for each employee per year of service);
- Depreciation of fixed assets under Ministry of Finance regulations;
- Enterprise management expenses;
- Interest payments on loans at rates below 1.2 times the current local commercial lending rate;

- Payments relating to education, training and healthcare activities, including subsidies to other local organizations/individuals;
- Salaries, allowances and social insurance paid for employees (including compulsory home-country social security contributions for expatriates, with proper documentation);
- Scientific and technical research expenses;
- Taxes, fees and assessments in the nature of tax;
- Travel allowances (limited as per regulations issued by the Ministry of Finance);
- Utility costs;
- Other expenses not exceeding 5 percent of total expenditure.

Examples of non-deductible items include:

- Accrued expenses;
- Advertising, promotion (except certain items), conferences/parties, commissions, prompt payment discounts, and costs exceeding 10 percent of the total of other expenses;
- Business management expenses allocated to permanent establishments in Vietnam by the foreign company which are not in accordance with the regulations;
- Costs of raw materials, energy, and fuel which are not reasonable;
- Depreciation of fixed assets which is not in accordance with the prevailing regulations (currently Decision 206);
- Employee remuneration expenses which are not stated in the labor contract or collective labor agreements;
- Life insurance premiums for employees;
- Penalties;
- Provisions for stock devaluation, bad debts, financial investment losses, warranty of products, goods or construction works which are not in accordance with regulations of the Ministry of Finance;
- Reserves for research and development not in accordance with regulations;
- Unrealized foreign exchange losses.

For certain businesses such as insurance companies, securities trading, and lotteries, the Ministry of Finance provides tailored regulations concerning deductible expenses for corporate income tax purposes.

Depreciation

According to Official Letter No. 817/TCT-CS dated February 15, 2008 on depreciation of fixed assets:

An item for depreciation of fixed assets may be included in reasonable expenses when calculating corporate income tax if the following conditions are satisfied:

a. The fixed assets are used for production, business and service activities;
b. The fixed assets have proper and complete invoices and vouchers proving ownership by the business establishment;
c. The fixed assets are managed, monitored and entered in the accounting books of the business establishment in accordance with the current regulations on management accounting.

Fixed assets which are not involved in business activities and which need not be depreciated includes other fixed assets which are not involved in business activities. Thus, where a Company was temporarily closed down in 2005 for three months due to the lack of raw materials and for maintenance and repair of machineries, it shall not be permitted to claim depreciation expense on the fixed assets which are not used in the business activities during such period.[3]

Unless a company obtains the approval of the Ministry of Finance, depreciation rates must be in accordance with Decision 206 of 2003. The decision allows for depreciation of all fixed assets contributed by foreign investment enterprises or foreign partners, including non-physical fixed assets, which include compensation and fees for the right to use land, patents and know-how. Foreign investment enterprises must use the straight-line method. This is calculated by taking the purchase or acquisition price of an asset subtracted by the salvage value divided by the total productive years the asset can be reasonably expected to benefit the company.

Normal depreciation rates for assets such as buildings, plants, equipment and vehicles depend on the estimated useful life of the asset. Typical life expectancies are 20 years for a hotel, exchange center or trade center; 7–15 years for a plant or mill; 5 years for equipment; and 5–7 years for vehicles. Annual depreciation rates are 5–15 percent for buildings, plants and architectural constructions; 10–25 percent for machinery and equipment; 15 percent for measuring and laboratory devices; 10–18 percent for a means of conveyance; 20–25 percent for office machinery and equipment; 33 percent for establishment costs, compensation for relocation, expenditures before production and non-physical fixed assets, such as know-how and patents; and 10–15 percent for other fixed assets.

Losses

Taxpayers may carry forward losses for five years. Tax losses may not be carried back. There is no provision for any form of group loss relief or consolidated filing.

Capital Gains Taxation

In 2008, gains by foreign companies on the transfer of interests in a foreign-invested or Vietnamese enterprise ("capital assignment") were subject to a flat tax of 28 percent. The taxable gain was determined as the excess of the sales proceeds less costs, less transfer expenses. The application of this tax is limited to changes of direct ownership of foreign investment enterprises.

Withholding Tax

Dividends

Vietnam does not levy withholding tax on dividends paid to residents or non-residents.

Interest

A 10 percent withholding tax is imposed on interest payments on offshore loans unless the rate is reduced under an applicable tax treaty.

Royalties

If the transfer of patents, technical know-how, technology processes or technical services is used as part of the capital contribution of a foreign investment enterprise, there is no tax related to the technology transfer. If it isn't a part of the capital contribution of the foreign investment enterprise, a foreign company transferring industrial-property rights as part of a licensing agreement is subject to a 10 percent tax on royalties.

Foreign Income and Tax Treaties

Vietnam has concluded a number of tax treaties, some of which are posted in Table 11.1. Since Vietnam did not impose withholding tax on dividends as of 2008, the table only sets out the tax rate on interest and royalties. Where such rates exceed 10 percent, only the 10 percent rate is stated to reflect the actual rate.

Transactions Between Related Parties

Transfer Pricing

The Ministry of Finance issued Circular 117/2005/TT-BTC in late 2005, which provided guidance to transactions between related parties, both within Vietnam and internationally, as well as transactions between the parent company outside of Vietnam and their Vietnamese branches. Generally, the circular aims to ensure that transactions by related companies follow the same guidelines as transactions by unrelated companies.

While Vietnam is not a member of the Organization for Economic Co-operation and Development (OECD), the transfer-pricing methods generally

Table 11.1   Withholding tax rates under tax treaties (percent)

Treaty partner	Interest	Royalties
Algeria	10	10
Australia	10	10
Belarus	10	10
Belgium	10	5/10
Bulgaria	10	10
Canada	10	7.5/10
China	10	10
Cuba	10	10
Czech Republic	10	10
Denmark	10	5/10
Finland	10	10
France	0	10
Germany	10	7.5/10
Hong Kong	10	7/10
Hungary	10	10
Iceland	10	10
India	10	10
Indonesia	10	10
Ireland	10	5/10
Italy	10	7.5/10
Japan	10	10
Korea (ROK)	10	5/10
Laos	10	10
Luxembourg	10	10
Malaysia	10	10
Mongolia	10	10
Myanmar	10	10
Netherlands	10	5/10
Norway	10	10
Pakistan	10	10
Philippines	10	10
Poland	10	1/10
Romania	10	10

Table 11.1 *(Continued)*

Treaty partner	Interest	Royalties
Russia	10	10
Singapore	10	5/10
Spain	10	10
Sweden	10	5/10
Switzerland	10	10
Taiwan	10	10
Thailand	10	10
Ukraine	10	10
United Kingdom	10	10
Uzbekistan	10	10

Source: Deloitte and PwC

follow those in the OECD guidelines, but with additional modifications and requirements. According to the tax experts at Deloitte Touche Tohmatsu,

> Vietnam's new transfer-pricing rules impose an onerous compliance burden on businesses with related-party transactions in Vietnam. The definition of related parties is very broad, and includes a control threshold of as low as 20 percent, which may be much lower than in many other countries. More importantly, the definition also covers significant supplies, purchases and lending relationships between otherwise unrelated parties. Related-party transactions must be identified and declared annually following prescribed forms that must be submitted together with the taxpayer's annual corporate income tax return. Businesses are required to make full self-assessment of their profits calculated on an arm's-length basis. In so doing, taxpayers are required to demonstrate that the pricing adopted is on arm's-length terms.
>
> Businesses are also required to maintain contemporaneous records—that is, records obtained and prepared at the time the related-party transactions took place, which serve as the basis for application of the methods of determining the arm's-length price. The contemporaneous records must include general information on the related-party relationships, transactional descriptions and diagrams, product technical specifications, contractual terms and conditions, and pricing

methodology. These documents must be available in Vietnamese and submitted to the tax authorities within 30 days of a request.

When a business enterprise does not follow the required transfer-pricing rules, the tax authorities may impose a deemed appropriate pricing or deem profits to be taxable or even apply a deemed tax. However, there are no administrative or specific transfer-pricing penalties stated in the rules, nor is there any mention of the possibility of obtaining an advance pricing agreement.[4]

Debt to Equity Proportion Requirements

Under the current Law on Investment, there is no restriction on capital or specific loan ratios (previously there was a minimum 30:70 percent ratio). When preparing a feasibility study and business plan, the investor must determine the relevant capital ratio to meet its business requirements. The licensing authority may review such ratios and make recommendations, but will not require the investor to change the capital ratio, unless it appears that the ratio is impractical.

Consolidated Returns

In many taxing jurisdictions around the world, as long as the parent company owns at least 80 percent of its affiliated companies, the companies can file a consolidated return. The filing of a consolidated return is generally not permitted in Vietnam. Each company in a group is required to file its own return.

Indirect Taxes and Duties

Value-added Tax (VAT)

VAT is imposed on the supply of goods and services at three rates: a standard rate of 10 percent and reduced rates of 0 percent and 5 percent. The 0 percent rate applies to export goods subject to special sales tax exports of software services to firms operating in export-processing zones goods processed by sub-contractors, and goods sold by a foreign investment enterprise to a foreign customer but delivered in Vietnam; and construction and installation activities for construction projects abroad. The 5 percent rate applies to approximately 41 types of goods and services. The 10 percent rate applies to 16 specific categories of goods and services, and a 17th catch-all group is defined as any good or service not subject to the other two rates.

Exempt from VAT are the export of services, including banking, finance and insurance. Other VAT-exempt categories include stock-exchange activities, certain imports, technology transfers, local sales of software products and services, services provided to consumers and firms outside Vietnam, and registration and insurance services for international means of transport.

Special VAT rules apply for companies in export-processing zones, although under WTO regulations tax incentives or holidays that constitute export performance requirements must be eliminated or phased out by January 2012. Such firms, also known as export-processing enterprises, do not pay VAT on imports; there is no withholding tax on services from foreign companies, and sales of goods from local companies (so-called "in country" exported goods) are zero-rated. The following goods and services sold to export-processing enterprises and to export-processing zones are subject to zero-rate VAT: accounting; auditing; banking; consulting; insurance; leasing of offices, houses and warehouses; posts; telecommunications; transport and warehousing; consumer goods and services for employees; and petroleum sold to means of transport.

According to KPMG, a monthly reporting procedure must be followed in order to maintain VAT compliance:

A monthly value-added tax declaration must be submitted with payment to the local tax office no later than the twentieth day of the following month. Within 90 days of the calendar or financial year end, a final value-added tax return must be submitted to the local tax office to finalize value-added tax for the year.

Any tax overpaid will be permitted to be carried forward to offset tax payable of the following months.[5]

Special Consumption Tax

A special consumption tax (SCT), also known as the special sales tax (SST), is levied on goods such as cigarettes and alcohol, vehicles with fewer than 24 seats, petrol, playing cards, joss paper (an item often burned during funerals) and some air conditioners.

An excise tax is levied on certain services, as well as their imports, at rates of 15–100 percent, based on the cost, insurance and freight price (the actual purchase price at destination, plus insurance and freight costs).

SST goods and services (with a few exceptions) are also subject to standard 10 percent VAT.

Accounting Standards

All business organizations incorporated in Vietnam (whether or not listed) are required to use the Ministry of Finance's Vietnamese Accounting Standards (VAS). Generally, the VAS is based on International Accounting Standards (IAS) that were issued up to 2003, although there are some modifications to reflect local accounting regulations and the local accounting environment (see Table 11.2). According to Deloitte Touche Tohmatsu, the Ministry of Finance is considering whether to grant rights to the Vietnam Association of Certified Public Accountants (VACPA) to formulate and update VAS. If this is formalized under the law, VACPA would then serve as the accounting standard setting body in Vietnam, rather than the Ministry of Finance.

Table 11.2 lists VAS in force as of August 2006.

The main requirements of VAS are:

- Companies must maintain charts of accounts, accounting vouchers and ledgers, financial reports and filing systems following prescribed methods.
- The account is normally maintained in Vietnamese dong. However, foreign-invested enterprises can maintain their account and issue their financial statements in a foreign currency through the prior registration with, and approval by, the MoF.

Table 11.2 Vietnamese Accounting Standards

VAS 01 Framework
VAS 02 Inventories
VAS 03 Tangible fixed assets
VAS 04 Intangible fixed assets
VAS 05 Investment property
VAS 06 Leases
VAS 07 Accounting for investments in associates
VAS 08 Financial reporting of interest in joint ventures
VAS 10 The effects of changes in foreign exchange rates
VAS 11 Business combinations
VAS 14 Revenues and other incomes
VAS 15 Construction contracts
VAS 16 Borrowing costs
VAS 17 Income taxes
VAS 18 Provisions, contingent liabilities and contingent assets
VAS 19 Insurance contracts
VAS 21 Presentation of financial statements
VAS 22 Disclosures in the financial statements of banks and
        similar financial institutions
VAS 23 Events after the balance sheet date
VAS 24 Cash flow statements
VAS 25 Consolidated financial statements and accounting for
        investments in subsidiaries
VAS 26 Related party disclosures
VAS 27 Interim financial reporting
VAS 28 Segment reporting
VAS 29 Changes in accounting policies, accounting estimates and errors
VAS 30 Earnings per share

- The financial year of foreign-invested enterprises must be the same as the tax year. The first fiscal year begins on the date of issue of the investment certificate.
- Foreign-invested enterprises can maintain their accounting system internally or by using the services of an independent accounting firm.[6]

All foreign-invested enterprises in Vietnam are required to have their financial statements audited by a qualified auditing firm. Audit firms are licensed and their activities are regulated by the Ministry of Finance.

The corporate income tax rate of 25 percent applies to all businesses except for oil and gas exploration and exploitation projects (on which a tax rate from 32 percent to 50 percent applies). Preferential rates apply under foreign investment incentives.

The business registration tax (also known as the commercial license tax) is VND1 million to VND3 million annually, depending on the type of business. Since foreign investment enterprises continue to receive investment licenses, only domestic firms pay the registration fee.

Businesses or individuals who carry out business activities in Vietnam outside existing regimens, such as the Common Investment Law (CIL, or Investment Law) or banking laws are generally referred to as "foreign contractors." Foreign contractors are subject to corporate income tax, value-added tax, special sales tax, import and export duties, and personal income tax.

Corporate Tax Administration

Tax administration is a burdensome task in Vietnam, as many processes are not automated and require significant effort. According to the tax experts at KPMG Vietnam:

Corporate entities must have a tax file number (called the Tax Code), except for those paying taxes on a withholding basis. Unless a business is granted special permission, it must use a calendar year for accounting and tax purposes.

Corporate entities must submit payment and lodge their returns to the tax agencies that directly manage them. CIT is calculated and payable on a quarterly basis in accordance with an establishment's declaration of corporate income tax or in accordance with the amount fixed by the tax office.

The tax office has the right to fix taxable income for the purpose of calculation of the amount of CIT payable by business establishments in the following cases:

- Failure to maintain, or adequately maintain books, invoices and source documents as required;
- Failure to declare, or accurately declare, the basis for the tax calculation or substantiate the contents of declaration forms as requested;
- Refusal to provide books of accounts, invoices, source documents and other necessary documents;
- If the business conducts activities without being registered.

On an annual basis, businesses must lodge a CIT finalization with the tax office within 90 days from the last day of the calendar year or financial year. If the amount of tax provisionally paid for the year is less than the total amount payable, the shortfall shall be paid within 10 days from the date of submitting the tax finalization. If the amount payable for the year is less than the amount provisionally paid, businesses may deduct such excess from the amount of tax payable in the next period.[7]

PERSONAL TAXATION

Residents in Vietnam are subject to tax on their worldwide income. An individual is resident if he/she has been in Vietnam for 183 days or more in a year. Foreigners who are present in Vietnam for 30 to 182 days in a calendar year are taxed on Vietnam-source income. Individuals in the country for less than 30 days are exempt from tax. As illustrated in Tables 11.3 and 11.4, prior to 2009, the personal income tax rate for residents and permanent foreigners ranged from 0 percent to 40 percent. As of 2009, the rates range from 0 percent to 35 percent.

As a general rule, payment of personal income tax is the legal responsibility of the employee, rather than the employer, but the obligation to withhold or pay the employee's personal income tax may rest with the employer initially. Where employees are given a gross wage, the employer will often withhold the personal income tax payable before making the wage payment to the employee, and remit the tax withheld to the state budget (via local tax departments or authorized agencies). If the employer pays employees on a net of tax basis, the employer is required to gross up the net income, calculate the applicable personal income tax and pay the tax due to the state budget.[8]

Table 11.3 Income tax rates prior to 2009

Income tax rates for foreigners employed in Vietnam

Average monthly receipts (VND millions)	Rate of taxation (percent)
0–8	0
8–20	10
20–50	20
50–80	30
80 and above	40

Income tax rates for Vietnamese employees

Average monthly receipts (VND millions)	Rate of taxation (percent)
0–5	0
5–15	10
15–25	20
25–40	30
40 and above	40

Source: Ministry of Finance

Table 11.4 Income tax rates as of 2009

Income tax rates for Residents, as of January 1, 2009

Average monthly receipts (VND millions)	Rate of taxation (percent)
0–5	0
5–10	10
10–18	15
18-32	20
32-52	25
52-80	30
Above 80	35

Source: Baker & McKenzie

Determination of Taxable Income Prior to 2009

Prior to 2009, tax rates for Vietnamese and expatriate residents in Vietnam were based on what is defined as regular income, which included:

- Wages and fees, including overtime salaries, third-shift salaries, extra-month(s) salaries or salaries received from the Social Insurance Fund, lunch allowances or meal allowances for a mid-shift break.
- Annual, quarterly and monthly bonuses, special bonuses for official and *Tet* holidays.
- Income from participation in business associations, a board of directors or board of management.
- Businesses or services not subject to corporate tax and income earned by individuals from activities such as construction design, consulting services under long-term contracts, training, teaching, examination coaching and cultural-artistic performances.
- House rents, electricity and water paid on the taxpayer's behalf, although house rents are taxable only up to 15 percent of an employee's salary.
- Income from the exercise of stock options and stock reward.

Certain fringe benefits, such as accommodation, utilities, use of a private car, schooling and transport while on leave, are considered part of the salary package and are thus taxable. The taxable value of employer-provided accommodation should be calculated as 15 percent of total taxable income. Certain categories of "income in kind" often earned by foreigners are exempt, including costs of repairing and equipping facilities for houses; bonuses in kind not exceeding one month's salary; tuition fees for children; and transport costs for home leave. These must be included in the employee's labor contract and paid by the employer to gain exemption.

Insurance-compensation payments paid to employees (for occupational accidents, serious diseases or death) are not taxable. However, insurance compensation received from non-compulsory insurance is subject to personal taxation as irregular income.

An exemption from interest withholding on bank deposits was available to foreign individuals.

Personal Income Taxes from January 1, 2009

Foreign companies operating in Vietnam are especially concerned about the changes to personal income taxation in 2009, especially if they are employing expatriates in the country or are comparing costs in Vietnam to costs in other Southeast Asian nations.

One reason for their concern is that even though the overall tax rates are lower for expatriates, the treatment of fringe benefits often given to assignees is now less favorable. As with many laws in Vietnam, the circulars try to clear up any fine details not covered in the law itself. Unfortunately, there are some important differences between Circular No. 81, which guides the implementation of the Ordinance on High Income Taxation, and Circular 84, which guides the implementation of PIT Law.

For example, home leave air tickets and dependent education are common benefit-in-kind items given to expatriates in Vietnam, and according to EuroCham Vietnam:

Circular 81 says that the expenses for air tickets, children's tuition, and relocation are not taxable income, while the expenses on accommodation leasing can enjoy a tax reduction. Meanwhile, Circular 84 says that all four kinds of expenses are all counted as taxable income.[9]

Thus, these items are now fully taxable, where the tax law was previously silent on the taxation of these perquisites.

Also, compared to other countries in Southeast Asia, the tax rates in Vietnam are high. For example, if a resident employee is making $100,000 equivalent in Hong Kong or Singapore, with a family size of four, the personal income tax paid would be about $8,000 per year. In Thailand, the employee would pay about $22,600 per year in taxes whereas in Vietnam, the employee would have to pay around $27,000.

In addition, where Vietnam was silent on the taxation of dividend income and capital gains prior to 2009, now these are treated as taxable income for both Vietnamese and foreign residents in Vietnam alike.

As of 2009, the following are now taxable in Vietnam:

- Dividends;
- Gains on sales of securities;
- Gains on sales of shareholdings in companies;
- Gains on sale of real estate (except single holdings of a house/land);
- Income from overseas remittances;
- Inheritances (in excess of VND10,000,000);
- Interest (except on bank deposits and life insurance policies).

Inheritance Tax

Prior to 2009, Vietnam did not have an inheritance tax. According to KPMG's 2008 *Taxation in Vietnam Guidebook*, as of January 1, 2009, with the exception of income being receipt of an inheritance of real property as between husband and wife; as between parents and children, including foster parents and adopted children; as between parents-in-law and children-in-law; as between grandparents and grandchildren; and as between siblings which is exempt, income from inheritances in excess of VND10,000,000 are subject to tax at the rate of 10 percent.

Gift Tax

Also prior to 2009, Vietnam did not have a gift tax. According to KPMG, as of January 1, 2009, with the exception of income being receipt of a gift of real property as between husband and wife; as between parents and children, including foster parents and adopted children; as between parents-in-law and children-in-law; as between grandparents and grandchildren; and as between siblings which is exempt, income from gifts in excess of VND10,000,000 are subject to tax at the rate of 10 percent.

TAX-RELATED RESOURCES

Please note: Vietnam's tax system is quite complex and requires considerable understanding in order to ensure compliance. Do not compute your business or personal taxes! Early 2009 was a time of great flux in the laws. In addition, the actual processes and procedures for ensuring compliance with many of the new tax laws are still being solidified. We strongly recommend that you seek counsel from a reputable tax or law firm regarding your particular situation.

Deloitte, PricewaterhouseCoopers and KPMG are qualified resources for anyone considering business in Vietnam, both from a tax compliance and tax planning perspective. Their contact information can be found below. Mr. Nguyen Thanh Vinh is an expert tax lawyer with Baker & McKenzie. His details also follow.

Deloitte Touche Tohmatsu
Hanoi Head Office – 8 Pham Ngoc Thach Rd., Dong Da District, Hanoi City,
     Tel: (84-4) 852 4123, Fax: (84-4) 852 4143, Email: tbui@deloitte.com
Ho Chi Minh City – 11th floor Sai Gon Trade Center, 37 Ton Duc Thang
     Street, District 1, Ho Chi Minh City, Tel: (84-8) 910 0751, Fax: (84-8)
     910 0750, Email: tdion@deloitte.com

KPMG

Ho Chi Minh City – 10th floor Sun Wah Tower, 115 Nguyen Hue Street, District 1, Ho Chi Minh City, Tel: (84-8) 3821 9266, Fax: (84-8) 821 9267, Email: kpmghcmc@kpmg.com.vn

Hanoi – 16th floor Pacific Place, 83B Ly Thuong Kiet Street, Hoan Kiem District, Hanoi, Tel: (84-4) 3946 1600, Fax: (84-4) 946 1601, Email: kpmghanoi@kpmg.com.vn

PricewaterhouseCoopers

Ho Chi Minh City – Level 4 Saigon Tower, 29 Le Duan Boulevard, District 1, Ho Chi Minh City, Tel: (84-8) 823 0796 Fax: (84-8) 825 1947

Hanoi – 7th floor Pacific Palace, 83B Ly Thuong Kiet Street, Hoan Kiem District, Hanoi, Tel: (84-4) 946 2246 Fax: (84-4) 946 0705

Baker & McKenzie

Ho Chi Minh City – 12th floor Saigon Tower, 29 Le Duan, District 1, Ho Chi Minh City, Tel: (84-8) 829 5585 Fax: (84-8) 829 5618, Email: thanhvinh.nguyen@bakernet.com

Other Resources:

Industrial Property Department (IDP)

1 Bis Yet Kieu, Hoan Kiem District, Hanoi,
Tel: (84-4) 8264707 or 8268737; Fax: (84-4) 8266185.

Market Management Bureau

59 Ly Tu Truong, District 1, Ho Chi Minh City,
Tel: (84-8) 8290677; Fax: (84-8) 8290674;
91 Dinh Tien Hoang, Hanoi;
Tel: (84-4) 8255502 or 8255834.

Ministry of Agriculture and Rural Development

2 Ngoc Ha, Ba Dinh District, Hanoi
Tel: (84-4) 8235804; Fax: (84-4) 8230381, http://www.agroviet.gov.vn

Ministry of Finance (MoF)

General Department of Taxation,
140 Nguyen Thi Minh Khai,
District 3, Ho Chi Minh City,
Tel: (84-8) 9330608,
http://www.gdt.gov.vn/gdtLive/?languageId=1&location=tct

Ministry of Industry

7 Trang Thi, Hanoi,
Tel: (84-4) 8253831, Fax: (84-4) 8265303,
http://www.industry.gov.vn (Vietnamese only).

Ministry of Labor, Invalids and Social Affairs (MoLISA)

12 Ngo Quyen, Hanoi,
http://www.molisa.gov.vn/gioithieu/introduce.asp

Ministry of Planning and Investment (MPI)

2 Hoang Van Thu Street, Hanoi,
Tel: (84-4) 8455298, 804-4404, Fax: (84-4) 8234453,
http://www.mpi.gov.vn

Office of the Government

1 Bach Thao, Hanoi,
Tel: (84-4) 8043279; Fax: (84-4) 8044130.

ENDNOTES

1. *Deloitte International Tax and Business Guide*, August 2007, http://www.
   deloitte.com/dtt/cda/doc/content/dtt_tax_guide_vietnam_121807.pdf
2. General Department of Taxation, Ministry of Finance, http://www.gdt.gov.vn/
   gdtLive/Trang-chu/Van-ban-phap-quy-ve-thue/News?contentId=1258858&
   location=tct
3. Grant Thornton Vietnam Tax Updates, January-February 2008, http://www.
   gt.com.vn/

4. *Deloitte International Tax and Business Guide*, August 2007, http://www.deloitte.com/dtt/cda/doc/content/dtt_tax_guide_vietnam_121807.pdf

5. *Taxation in Vietnam* 2008 Edition, KPMG, http://www.kpmg.com.vn/files/TaxationVietnamJun08.pdf

6. Living in Vietnam Investment and Tax Guide, http://www.livinginvietnam.com/US_Version/BusinessinVietnam.htm

7. *Taxation in Vietnam* 2008 Edition, KPMG, http://www.kpmg.com.vn/files/TaxationVietnamJun08.pdf

8. Ibid.

9. "Enterprises will have to pay more to employ foreign employees," Vietnam Business Finance Information for Successful Investment, http://www.vnbusinessnews.com/2009/01/enterprises-will-have-to-pay-more-to.html

Epilogue—Can You Handle the Truth?

So many of our early days were spent shaking our heads, wringing our hands, crying and generally feeling shocked with what we were faced with on a daily basis. And this was not our first stop in the developing world, as Brian spent years in remote Tanzania. No matter where you've been, or what nationality you are, nothing you've experienced is exactly like what you'll experience in Vietnam. Guaranteed.

We broke this book into the three areas which we felt were most crucial to the successful construction and execution of a Vietnam-proof business plan. We also structured it this way because most of your crucial decision making will neatly fall into one of these three categories; Get Ready, Get Set or Go! And yes, it is a bit of a race, but more of a marathon than a sprint.

As you are aware, Vietnam offers a wealth of opportunities. Its economy is one of the fastest growing in Asia, and the people are hard working, spirited and steadfastly determined to improve their standard of living. The country's track record of recent success is impressive and shows little signs of letting up. Coupled with this great opportunity comes a difficult environment to live in. The country is developing. It has problems with air, water and other environmental pollution. There are health risks and the education system requires foreign children to be put into expensive international schools. This lack of development extends to the infrastructure throughout the country as well. It can create prohibitive logistical challenges for some companies. Government relations and regulations also prove to be a challenge for many.

Once the decision has been made to venture into the Vietnam market, the advice and experience of many who have gone before counsel thorough research and an understanding of what should be done prior to arriving in the country. Understanding the competitive landscape and how you are going to operate within this environment is crucial. It must be remembered that the country has had a very intense recent history. Consequently, the culture is unique and having an open mind to understanding it will contribute to a more effective approach to dealing with competitors, having a fruitful relationship with local partners, and satisfying the domestic consumer.

Most importantly, there are going to be lots of obstacles in this adventure. That should be both part of the challenge and part of the fun. With the right attitude, the myriad of strange rules, regulations and ways of doing things can become part of the spice of life. With the wrong attitude these obstacles will both drive you crazy and consume your time, energy and resources.

Unfortunately, there are far more stories of failure than of success. But there are success stories. On the plus side, because Vietnam's business environment is so difficult to navigate, it acts as a serious barrier to entry for your competitors. And you now have the collective wisdom of many experts at your fingertips, as well as important details about how to protect yourself and stay in compliance.

This book is really about making dreams come true. So many Westerners conjure up images of a war-torn country when asked what comes to mind when they hear the word "Vietnam." And for some Vietnamese, especially from the North, they might first see a soldier in their mind's eye when asked to conjure up an image of a Westerner. These old images need to be replaced with new, more mutually flattering and productive ones.

Today, the Vietnamese are dreaming of development, of fostering cooperative relationships with the world, and of furthering investment in their beautiful country. We dreamed, like many do, of helping Vietnam in our own small way: of making a positive contribution while also making a living. We hope that you too will realize your dreams and we wish you great success in tomorrow's market today!

Industrial and Economic Sector Overview

Some industries and economic sectors offer more opportunity than others. Here are some that have good potential:

EXPORT PRODUCTION

Like many newly developed countries, such as Taiwan and South Korea, Vietnam welcomed the large contract manufacturers that produce for Nike and Adidas in the early 1990s. This action attracted many apparel and shoe manufacturers, followed by light and heavy manufacturing including auto manufacturers such as Toyota.

There are opportunities for small, medium and large-scale production, using an already established operation to handle your company orders or for setting up a dedicated plant. Currently, the biggest challenges to operating a manufacturing center in Vietnam are human resources, transportation and inflation.

Despite these serious concerns, many entities have decided that Vietnam is still a destination of choice for manufacturing, as compared to other countries. Intel, for example, chose Vietnam over China for a $300 million chip assembly and testing factory. Choosing Vietnam was based on several factors, but an important one was that in China, Intel would be a little fish in a very big pond. This project was also relatively more important for Vietnam to secure, by comparison. Intel hopes that this means they have the ear of the government, and that the government will partner willingly with Intel in order to make the investment a huge success. Based on the large size of the investment, this may be the case.

AGRICULTURAL SECTOR

Agricultural sector products such as feed and fertilizers, which increase yields per acre, will become popular imports to Vietnam, as arable land per capita is low in comparison to other Asian locations. Also, as personal income continues to rise for most Vietnamese, the demand for imported food and drink should also increase. Protein demand typically increases as wealth increases, which bodes well for foreign meat producers interested in selling in Vietnam.

Vietnam's furniture and textiles sectors are expanding rapidly, which holds promise for domestic raw materials producers and for manufacturers in these sectors.

POWER GENERATION AND RELATED SERVICES/PRODUCTS

According to Vietnam's Sixth Power Development Master Plan, growth in electricity demand is expected to increase dramatically from now until 2025, and the state-owned monopoly, Electricity of Vietnam (EVN), is ill-equipped to meet the increased demand. In 2006, the International Finance Corporation (IFC) and the Ministry of Industry signed a financial advisory agreement to increase the number of Independent Power Projects (IPPs) that are open for foreign investment.[1]

Some areas that offer good opportunities include:

• Consulting and engineering services, including project management;
• Installation and construction services;

- Machinery, equipment and materials;
- Low, medium and high voltage electrical equipment for the national grid;
- Low and medium voltage electrical equipment for industry, institutions and households;
- Supply of equipment, spare parts, materials, consumables, and overhaul and maintenance services (after-market);
- Investment in new IPP power projects in the form of build, operate, and transfer (BOT); build and transfer (BT); build, transfer and operate (BTO); and joint-venture (JV).

Sample energy projects that may provide opportunities for energy companies and professionals include:

- Second Transmission and Distribution Project II funded by the World Bank ($200 million) and the Vietnamese government, for a total project amount of $327.8 million (approved in July 2005 and to be completed in December 2010). (For more information, visit: www.worldbank.org.am/external/default/main?pagePK=64027221&piPK=64027220&theSitePK=301579&menuPK=301612&Projectid=P084871)
- Northern Rural Power Project funded by the Asian Development Bank ($120 million), the French Development Agency (EUR40 million) and the Vietnamese government ($103 million). This project was approved in August 2005 and is to be completed in June 2009. (For more information, visit:www.adb.org/Documents/Profiles/LOAN/32273013.ASP)

CONSTRUCTION

Spending in the construction sector is expected to grow at a compound annual growth rate (CAGR) of 5.5 percent, from $805 million in 2005 to $1,369 million in 2015. With an expected growth in population of approximately 860,000 per year and increasing personal incomes, the residential construction market offers promising prospects. Spending in the residential construction sector is expected to increase at a CAGR of 4.2 percent from $398 million in 2005 to $603 million in 2015.

Commercial real estate including office buildings and industrial construction are also growth areas in Vietnam. Non-residential construction spending may grow at a CAGR of 6.5 percent, from $407 million in 2005 to $766 million in 2015. Government policies, such as the modernization of customs services, privatization of SOEs, and encouragement of foreign direct investment, create a favorable non-residential construction industry outlook.[2]

TELECOMMUNICATIONS EQUIPMENT AND SERVICES

With Vietnam's accession to the WTO limitations on foreign companies that provide telecommunications services will be less restrictive, resulting in increased opportunity for foreign investment, and increased competition. In the past, foreign telecom companies were involved mainly as suppliers of equipment in the building of network infrastructure for Vietnam Post and Telecom (VNPT), the dominant state-owned provider.

In Vietnam's "Strategy for Development of ICT Industries to 2010 with Orientation to 2020," it is predicted that by 2010 Vietnam's information and communication technologies industries will achieve an annual growth rate of 20–25 percent and annual revenue of $6-7 billion. Telecom entrants (non-VNPT) will achieve a 40–50 percent market share.

Thus, foreign telecommunications companies should be able to find opportunities in almost every facet of the telecommunications equipment and services industry, from equipment for building the infrastructure, to value-added services.[3]

Vietnam's telecommunications equipment and services market information is listed in Table A1.1; the country's major buyers for telecommunications equipment and services are listed in Table A1.2:[4]

Table A1.1 Telecommunications equipment and services market information

In millions of USD	2006 (actual)	2007 (estimated)	2008 (estimated)
	Telecommunications Equipment		
Market Size	1,650	2,060	2,575
Local Production	529	735	920
Exports	24	30	38
Imports	1,085	1,350	1,688
	Telecommunications Services		
Market Size	2,571	3,200	4,000
Local Production	2,669	3,330	4,125
Exports	285	355	443
Imports	187	230	287

Source: Unofficial Industry Estimates

OIL AND GAS SERVICES/MACHINERY

The government of Vietnam is encouraging investments in offshore oil and gas exploration from both domestic and foreign entities. Under its commitments to the WTO, the oil and gas sector as a whole is open to foreign companies that can bring in capital, expertise and technologies to help achieve the country's major development goals. The government has made tremendous headway in attracting foreign companies, by enacting an amended Petroleum Law in 2000, implementing major management reforms in PetroVietnam, and cracking down on business malpractices including corruption, graft, and embezzlement. Foreign oil and gas companies active and successful in Vietnam include ConocoPhillips, BP, Chevron-Unocal, Talisman, KNOC (Korea), ONGC Vadesh (India), Idemitsu (Japan), Zarubezneft (Russia), and PETRONAS Carigalli (Malaysia).

This new, more open business environment has undoubtedly generated a steadily increasing demand for equipment and services that will continue in

Table A1.2 Major buyers for telecommunication equipment and services

	Fixed telephone service operators	International telecommunications service operators	Telephone service based on internet protocol (IP) operators	Mobile communications service operators	Internet services providers
Electricity of Vietnam (EVN Telecom)	●		●		●
Hanoi Telecommunications Company (Hanoi Telecom)	●		●		●
FPT Group	●	●	●	●	●
Military Electronics Telecommunications Corporation (Viettel)				●	
Netnam Company (Netnam)					●
One-Connection Internet Service Joint Stock Company (OCI)					●
Saigon Post and Telecommunications Service (SPT or Saigon Post)	●		●	●	●
Trade Import Export Company (Tienet—TIE)			●		●
Vietnam Maritime Communications and Electronics Company (Vishipel)	●	●			
Vietnam Posts and Telecommunications Group (VNPT)	●	●	●	●	●

Source: 2009 Country Commercial Guide—US Commercial Service

the years to come. It is estimated that the oil and gas industry will require an investment of about $28-31 billion to achieve the goals set forth by the government for the period 2006–2025. Table A1.3 details the estimated investment in the various sub-sectors of the industry, which can give you an indication of the opportunities available in each sub-sector.

Thus, according to PetroVietnam's 2006 estimates, investments in the oil and gas industry over the next 20 years are expected to more than double in order to keep pace with domestic and foreign demands. The strength of this sector means that opportunities exist in the provision of the following oil- and gas-related products and services:

- Blowout preventers (BOPs);
- Chemicals and lubricants;
- Corrosion and abrasion controllers;
- Cranes, hoists, and winches;
- Deep-sea drilling services and equipment;
- Enhanced recovery equipment services;
- Gas industry building construction;
- Geophysical survey services and equipment;
- Industry-related computer and wireless technologies;
- Instruments and control systems;
- Logging and formation evaluation;
- Marine equipment and services;
- Offshore engineering and design services;
- Offshore fixed and floating platforms;
- Offshore technology licensing;
- Perforating and testing services;
- Pollution, oil spill control, and environmental;
- Power supply, engines, and turbines;
- Process equipment;
- Production equipment and services;
- Project management services;
- Pumps and compressors;

Table A1.3 Estimated investment in the oil and gas industry for the 2006–2025 period

Investment Projects	Total Investment US$ million	Total Value (PV's Share)	Total Funding		
			2006–2010	2011–2015	2016–2025
Exploration, field development & production	8,790–10,730	2,070–2,620	2,430–3,010	2,310–2,920	4,050–4,800
Gas collection & transport	1,983–2,483	1,233–1,483	760	723–973	500–750
Total investment in offshore operations	**10,773–13,213**	**3,303–4,103**	**3,190–3,770**	**3,033–3,893**	**4,550–5,550**
Overseas oil exploration & production	3,070–4,000	2,660–3,475	470–600	900–1,300	1,700–2,100
Petroleum processing	10,510	6,305	3,040	3,370	4,100
Petroleum products distribution & sales	1,970–2,070	1,970–2,071	1,260	260–310	450–500
Petroleum services & trading	1,680	1,680	1,125	500	55
Total Investment	**28,003–31,473**	**15,918–17,634**	**9,085–9,795**	**8,063–9,373**	**10,855–12,305**

Source: PetroVietnam 2006

174

- Retrieval and fishing tools;
- Ropes, wire ropes, and chains;
- Rubber products;
- Software engineering services and equipment;
- Tools;
- Tubes and piping;
- Valves and actuators;
- Well-completion equipment and services;
- Well-head assemblies.

AIRPORT SUPPORT SERVICES AND EQUIPMENT

Vietnam's government recognizes that rapid national economic growth requires an adequate transportation infrastructure, and aviation is a key component. The Civil Aviation Administration of Vietnam (CAAV), a government agency reporting to the Ministry of Transport, has responsibility for overseeing the development of Vietnam's aviation industry.

Vietnam Airlines is the country's flagship carrier, serving over 6.8 million passengers in 2006, the same year in which the total airport through-put of passengers reached 16 million. Vietnam's airport traffic is expected to rise to over 20 million passengers by 2010.

According to CAAV, as of May 2007, there were 35 airlines other than Vietnamese carriers with regularly scheduled flights servicing Vietnam. The country currently operates a network of 21 major civil airports including three international airports: the Noi Bai Airport in the north of the country (Hanoi), Danang in the center and Tan Son Nhat in the south (Ho Chi Minh City). The Tan Son Nhat airport handles about 70 percent of the country's international passenger traffic.

CAAV estimated in 2007 that they would require approximately $15 billion to achieve their development plan for the aviation sector by 2020. Of this, $8 billion will be needed mainly for aircraft fleet expansion, $5 billion for constructing and upgrading airports and the remaining $2 billion for airport operation and air traffic management. Vietnam's airports are in need of a facelift. The quality of the facilities at the International Airport in Danang, for example, is currently in far worse condition than neighboring Cambodia's Siem Reap International Airport. Siem Reap's airport is pleasant, efficient and has adequate seating for passengers waiting for their flight. Danang's Airport is by comparison, run-down, dingy and too small.

In addition to the airport issues from a passenger perspective, foreign airlines have complained of an unfair business environment. Service charges at Vietnam's airports increased sharply in early 2008, making Vietnam a more expensive destination for airlines to land their aircraft, as compared to neighboring countries. Part of the complaint also stems from preferential fuel pricing only for Vietnam Airlines.[5] Only time will tell if Vietnam's airport authorities are willing to make real and long-term changes that are necessary to attract foreign money and accommodate foreign travel.

The airport expansion and renovation plan for the period 2005–2010 calls for investment of more than $1.3 billion, in order to accomplish an efficient network of 21 airports in operation, including projects such as Noi Bai (second terminal), Na San, Dong Hoi, Cam Ranh, Chu Lai, Lien Khuong, Con Dao, Phu Quoc (International), Can Tho, Ca Mau, and Rach Gia. From 2010 to 2020, several other airports will be constructed or upgraded including Long Thanh (International), Chu Lai (Cargo), Cat Bi (Hai Phong), Quang Ninh (International), Lao Cai, and Cao Bang. Most of the investment in airport projects is expected to be financed by the Official Development Assistance (ODA) loans from foreign governments, such as Japan, as well as the private sector.

Foreign aviation and airport ground services-related companies will find opportunities for providing architectural, engineering and construction services, as well as construction management services for airports and terminals. Opportunities also exist in supplying airport ground support equipment, equipment for passenger terminals, air traffic management systems, telecommunication systems, aircraft parts, training services, as well as aircraft maintenance and engine overhaul services.[6]

ENVIRONMENTAL SERVICES

According to Vietnam's Directorate for Standards and Quality,

Outdated technology and lack of proper treatment facilities generate large quantities of air emission, waste water and hazardous wastes. The industrial pollution is concentrated in Hanoi, Ho Chi Minh City, Dong Nai, Vung Tau, Hai Phong, Quang Ninh, Vinh Phu and Quang Nam-Da Nang. In Ho Chi Minh City, Hanoi, and Viet Tri Township of Vinh Phu province, the concentrations of dust, particulate matters and unhealthy substances in ambient air exceed World Health Organization (WHO) environmental standards guidelines. Most of the liquid effluents are discharged to recipient waters without proper treatment. Aware of these problems, the government of Vietnam has already taken several steps to improve the situation, mainly through:

- Establishing a National Environmental Agency (1993) under the Ministry of Science, Technology and Environment (MOSTE) to coordinate environmental protection activities in Vietnam;
- Approving an Environmental Protection Law in January 1994;
- Establishing more than 80 environmental standards released in 1995 (ambient air and water quality standards, air emission and effluent standards);
- Creating an Environmental Unit in the Ministry of Planning and Investment;
- Requiring the Ministry of Planning and Investment to conduct an environmental review before approving foreign investment;
- Creating the Department of Science, Technology and Environment in each of Vietnam's provinces and cities in charge of reviewing investments' environmental aspects and resolving pollution-related disputes.[7]

Many opportunities are available for consulting with government and businesses on meeting these environmental criteria. The sale of equipment for the effective management of waste is another area that is experiencing high growth in Vietnam.

HEALTH CARE

According to WHO,

> The health system in Vietnam is a mixed public-private provider system, in which the public system still plays a key role in health care, especially in prevention, research and training. The private sector has grown steadily since the reform of the health sector in 1989, but is mainly active in outpatient care; inpatient care is provided essentially through the public sector. Only 26 percent of private health facilities participate in primary health care activities. In treatment areas, specialized hospitals and clinics account for only 11.36 percent of health facilities and are therefore often overloaded. The ratio of nurses to doctors is still very low.[8]

Health care is strengthened by national health programs, especially those for important public health problems. The tuberculosis control program is now considered to be one of the best, with treatment success rates of more than 90 percent. However, coverage in poor communities and mountainous areas is limited to 50–60 percent of the population.

An extended immunization program is also considered to be a successful child health care program, as evidenced by a high reduction in vaccine-preventable diseases, the elimination of polio, and gradual elimination of newborn tetanus. However, current conditions for vaccine maintenance, vaccination timing and safety, and high staff turnover are among the challenges to the continued quality of child immunization.

The total health expenditure in 2005 was 6 percent of GDP (see Table A1.4). Government expenditure accounts for only 25.7 percent, the majority of which is allocated to treatment, with increasing rates from 71.29 percent in 1991 to 85.02 percent in 2000. Budget allocation rates for prevention remain low and continue to decrease. Generally speaking, health insurance policies have not been implemented in the private sector. Policies are being implemented to address the needs of the poor including health insurance

Table A1.4   Health care expenditure indicators

Indicator	Value (2005)
External resources for health as percentage of total expenditure on health	2.0
General government expenditure on health as percentage of total expenditure on health	25.7
General government expenditure on health as percentage of total government expenditure	5.1
Out-of-pocket expenditure as percentage of private expenditure on health	86.10
Per capita government expenditure on health at average exchange rate ($)	10.0
Per capita government expenditure on health (Purchasing Power Parity (PPP) $)	57.0
Per capita total expenditure on health (PPP $)	221.0
Per capita total expenditure on health at average exchange rate ($)	37.0
Private expenditure on health as percentage of total expenditure on health	74.3
Private prepaid plans as percentage of private expenditure on health	2.5
Social security expenditure on health as percentage of general government expenditure on health	33.5
Total expenditure on health as percentage of gross domestic product	6.0

Source: World Health Organization

cards, direct exemption from hospitalization fees, and the establishment of health care funds but with limited coverage because of budget shortages.

Currently, the most pressing issues are improving the quality of care, the number of qualified healthcare staff and training health staff, and increasing public funding for health care through extension of health insurance coverage. Inequity is highest in outpatient and rehabilitation services. A large disparity in access to health care facilities exists across regions and population groups, particularly in mountainous areas and among minority ethnic groups and the poor. Access to blood transfusion services is also difficult in many parts of the country and paid blood donors are still the main sources of blood for transfusion. The volume of blood collected, even from the paid donors, does not meet the needs of patients.[9]

The Ministry of Health's development plan (2006–2010) estimates $1.8 billion should be spent to build and equip 57 new hospitals of which over $1 billion is set aside for medical equipment. Many non-governmental organizations (NGOs) will fund or loan funds for this endeavor. Epidemic prevention drives and medical check-ups for the poor are two other areas being funded by NGOs. These projects address HIV/AIDS prevention and care, in addition to other important projects.

Thus, significant opportunities exist for pharmaceutical companies, medical insurers, medical equipment suppliers, hospital/healthcare professionals/consultants and medical training service providers in Vietnam. Major health-related project information can be found via the World Bank and the Asian Development Bank websites.

EDUCATION AND TRAINING

As in many other Asian countries, education and higher education degrees rank high on the to-do list for most Vietnamese. There are many opportunities for foreign educators and education-related companies, from teaching English to running corporate training and development consultancies. While the market is beginning to see several new companies, there is still plenty of room in the booming educational sector.

Vietnam's 2001–2010 Education Development Strategy and Vision aims to raise the quality of education offered via the public school system. This is a good goal, considering the many shortcomings of the current system: much of the curriculum is outdated; school classrooms are over-crowded and teachers foster a system where the most important lessons are provided only for those students who take extra-tuition private classes from them outside the regular school day.

Given these realities, multinationals are looking for more creative solutions to improve the skills of incoming employees. One interesting entry strategy for schools or training institutions is seeking a partnership with a multinational corporation or a group of company sponsors, to deliver education and training that addresses the lack of knowledge and critical skills needed by their new employees. Some needs include: management and other soft skills training (that is, leadership, cooperative communication, creative problem solving, effective teamwork skills, and so on), English or other foreign language acquisition, technical skills and vocational training especially in the booming information technology sector.

FRANCHISING

In 2006, the government released decree No. 35/2006/ND-CP. This decree addressed franchising and provided legal guidance for franchise agreements and government administration of franchises. Given this and the youthful, urban demographic with increasing disposable income, franchising could be a very lucrative enterprise. Some of the more promising opportunities for franchises include convenience stores and food and beverage outlets. It is important to adjust the franchise fee arrangement to suit Vietnamese market levels, if having many stores throughout Vietnam is the first concern.

Franchise registration is conducted by the Ministry of Trade and Industry. The franchise must be registered either with the Ministry of Trade and Industry, or the Provincial Department of Trade, in the province from which the franchise will be administered.

INFORMATION TECHNOLOGY

While Table A1.5 indicates that the future looks bright for all things computer-related, most buying in Vietnam (approximately 80 percent) has been hardware-related and software piracy runs rampant. Vietnam's software infringement rates in 2006 were 88 percent, down from 92 percent in 2004. Enforcement of newly enacted intellectual property rights laws is now seen on the streets, whereas just years ago you could see stalls openly selling

Table A1.5   Growth in IT industry investment

In millions of USD	2006 (actual)	2007 (estimated)	2008 (estimated)
	Total IT Hardware and Software Market		
Market Size	1,740	2,260	2,940
Exports	1,233	1,600	2,083
Imports	1,412	1,835	2,386

Source: Estimates based on 2007 Vietnam IT Industry Outlook Annual Report, Ho Chi Minh City Computer Association

pirated Microsoft XP disks for about $1 each. While there are still pirated and counterfeit software suppliers in the market, they are now more discreet.

ENDNOTES

1. Electricity Commission of Vietnam's english language Site, http://www.evn.com.vn/Trangchủ/tabid/59/language/en-US/Default.aspx
2. Geoffrey Lubien, "Construction spending analysis and forecast for Vietnam," Global Insight's Advisory Services, http://www.construction-int.com/categories/vietnam-construction-market/vietnam-construction-market.asp
3. Vietnam's Ministry of Post and Telematics, http://mic.gov.vn/details_e.asp?Object=271032875&news_ID=13648450
4. "Commercial Guide for Conducting Business in Vietnam," U.S. Commercial Service, http://www.buyusa.gov/vietnam/en/country_commercial_guide.html
5. "Aviation sector firms complaints gain wings," *Vietnam Investment Review*, April 2008, http://www.vir.com.vn/Client/VIR/index.asp?url=content.asp&doc=16155
6. "Commercial Guide for Conducting Business in Vietnam," US Commercial Service, http://www.buyusa.gov/vietnam/en/country_commercial_guide.html
7. "Directorate for Standards and Quality, Vietnam," http://www.tcvn.gov.vn/en/index.php
8. "Country Cooperation Strategy: Vietnam 2003-2006," World Health Organization, http://www.who.int/countryfocus/cooperation_strategy/ccs_vnm_en.pdf
9. Ibid.

Vietnam Living Conditions

SEVERE CLIMATE

For life in Ho Chi Minh City, "sweaty" is the most appropriate year-round description. If you are accustomed to changing seasons, brace yourself for life in this land of eternal summer heat and humidity. Ho Chi Minh City has a tropical climate that is hot and humid enough to cause discomfort for at least six months of the year. Average temperatures range from 21°C to 32°C (70°F to 89°F) in January and from 24°C to 31°C (75°F to 88°F) in July. Frequent downpours occur during the rainy season from May through November, and then the dry season from December to April remains hot and humid. Annual rainfall averages 1,983 millimeters (78 inches). The city lies approximately two-and-a half meters (eight feet) above sea level, making floods a hazard during the rainy season.[1] Hanoi's weather, on the other hand, varies; from hot and humid summers to bone-chilling winds from China in the winter. According to the Vietnam National Administration of Tourism,

Hanoi is situated in a tropical monsoon zone with two main seasons. During the dry season, which lasts from October to April, it is cold and there is very little rainfall, except from January to March, when the weather is still cold but there is some light rain. The wet season, from May to September, is hot with heavy rains and storms. The average annual temperature is 23.2°C (73.7°F) and the average annual rainfall is 1,800mm (71 inches). The average temperature in winter is 17.2°C (62.9°F), but can go down to 8°C (46.4°F). The average temperature in summer is 29.2°C (84.6°F), but can reach up to 39°C (102.2°F).[2]

POLLUTION, SANITATION ISSUES AND DISEASE

Raw sewage and untreated industrial waste pollute the waterways. The air in the cities is filled with motorbike and automobile exhaust. WHO warns that Ho Chi Minh City's sulfur dioxide, nitrogen dioxide and particulate matter are all above their guidelines. As a result of the less than satisfactory state of air and water quality, upper respiratory disorders, tuberculosis and hepatitis are common in Vietnam. For people with weakened immunity or an existing or chronic illness, these factors could become life-threatening. It is absolutely vital for anyone venturing to Vietnam to prevent exposure to many communicable diseases by washing hands frequently, washing food thoroughly, peeling fresh fruits, boiling all tap water before using it in cooking, and drinking bottled water exclusively.[3]

Many mosquito-borne illnesses are also endemic to Vietnam, including Japanese encephalitis, dengue fever, and malaria. While it isn't necessary to sleep under mosquito nets in the major cities, it is wise to use them in outlying areas and to apply insect repellant liberally especially during dusk and dawn. In the major cities, fogging of mosquitoes is commonplace.

According to a 2008 ORC Worldwide report,

To date Vietnam has a total of 100 human cases of avian influenza, of which 46 were fatal. The majority of cases were in 2005; in 2007 there were at least seven human cases reported in the country, along with widespread outbreaks in poultry. Recommended precautions for expatriates include avoiding poultry farms and live bird markets, and any surface that may be contaminated by bird feces or secretions, and thoroughly cooking all poultry-based foods, including eggs.[4]

VACCINATION SCHEDULE FOR SHORTER STAYS (LESS THAN FOUR WEEKS)

The Family Medical Practice recommends the following vaccinations for short-term and long-term residents in Vietnam:[5]

Hepatitis A

The hepatitis A virus (HAV) is a liver disease that can affect anyone. Immunization is recommended, as the disease is easily contracted through contaminated food and infected food handlers. The vaccination consists of two injections separated by six months. You are considered immunized two weeks after the first shot; however, for long-lasting immunity, you should complete the second shot after six months.

Typhoid

Typhoid fever is a life-threatening illness, caused by the bacterium *Salmonella Typhi*. Typhoid fever is not a tropical disease and is related to hygiene and sanitary conditions, rather than the climate itself. A typhoid vaccination is particularly important because of the presence of *Salmonella Typhi* strains that are resistant to multiple antibiotics in this region. It is found in many types of contaminated food and water. The typhoid vaccination consists of one vaccination, followed by a booster shot every three years.

Hepatitis B

The hepatitis B virus (HBV) is a serious disease that can cause lifelong infections, liver cancer, liver failure, and even death. HBV is spread by contact with bodily fluids, such as semen, blood, vaginal and anal secretions, urine and saliva; or it can be caught by receiving a contaminated blood transfusion or other medical product. A hepatitis B vaccination is recommended for everyone, especially those who may be exposed to blood (for example, healthcare workers), have sexual contact with the local population, or stay longer than six months in Asia. The hepatitis B vaccine is also recommended for all infants and for children who did not complete the series as infants.

The primary hepatitis B series consists of three shots: the first two injections should be one month apart, and the third injection should be six months after the initial vaccination. More than 90 percent of people become immunized after the second shot; however, for long-lasting immunity, a third shot should be completed after six months. One booster shot is necessary every five years.

VACCINATION SCHEDULE FOR LONGER STAYS (MORE THAN FOUR WEEKS)

Japanese Encephalitis

The Japanese encephalitis virus is transmitted by infected mosquito bites to humans, causing inflammation of the brain, leading to permanent brain damage, neurological deficiencies and high mortality rates. Immunization is recommended only if you plan to visit rural areas for four weeks or more, and in areas with known outbreaks of the virus. All children staying in Vietnam for more than four weeks should be immunized against Japanese encephalitis, which consists of three shots: the first two vaccinations should be one week apart, and the third one, 28 days after the initial vaccination. One booster shot is recommended every three to four years.

Rabies

Rabies is a preventable viral disease that causes acute encephalitis (inflammation of the brain). The virus exists in the saliva of mammals and is transmitted from animal to animal or from animal to human by biting and/or scratching. The virus can also be spread by licking; when infected saliva contacts open cuts or wounds and the mouth, eyes, and nose. A rabies vaccination is recommended if you may be exposed to wild or domestic animals through work or recreation. It consists of three shots: the first two injections should be from one to two weeks apart and the third, 28 days after the initial injection.

Tuberculosis (TB)

Tuberculosis (TB) is a disease caused by the bacterium *Mycobacterium Tuberculosis*, which usually affects the respiratory system, but can also affect other parts of the body, such as the kidneys, spine and brain and can be fatal if not treated properly. One vaccination is required for children under the age of five.

Other Diseases

Family Medical Practice also recommends booster doses of other vaccines:

- Tetanus-diphtheria every ten years;
- Polio every ten years;
- Flu shot (influenza virus) annually.

WHO recommends a flu shot to combat the avian flu, which is also known as bird flu.

INADEQUATE MEDICAL FACILITIES/QUESTIONABLE PHARMACEUTICAL PRODUCTS

Vietnam lacks high quality healthcare in areas outside of Hanoi or Ho Chi Minh City. In one visit to a rural hospital, an inspection noted one shared cup for all sick people at the water cooler, neither soap nor toilet paper in any of the bathrooms, crumbling paint on the walls, dirty floors, and mattresses without bed linens.

Expatriates are advised to use the private clinics in Ho Chi Minh City or Hanoi for routine care, such as Family Medical Practice or International SOS. There are also French hospitals in both Hanoi and Ho Chi Minh City with adequate care for most medical procedures. For major health issues, a medical evacuation to Bangkok or Singapore is recommended.

While pharmacies in Ho Chi Minh City and Hanoi generally carry a better supply of pharmaceutical products than do those in other Vietnamese cities, some sell drugs that may be counterfeit, outdated, or improperly stored. You are advised to purchase drugs at a reputable pharmacy—one affiliated with an international clinic, for example.

CRIME

According to the U.S. Department of State,

Cities in Vietnam have the crime problems typical of many other large cities throughout the world. Pick-pocketing and other petty crimes occur regularly. Although violent crimes such as armed robbery are still relatively rare in Vietnam, perpetrators have grown increasingly bold, and the U.S. Consulate General has received recent reports of knives and razors being used in attempted robberies in Ho Chi Minh City. Thieves congregate around hotels frequented by foreign tourists and business people. Assaults have also been reported in outlying areas. The evolving violent nature of incidents warrants caution. Motorcyclists are known to snatch bags, cameras and other valuables from pedestrians or passengers riding in "cyclos" (pedicabs) or riding on the back of rented motorcycles. Serious injuries have resulted when thieves snatched purses or bags that were strapped across their victims' bodies, resulting in the victim being dragged along the ground by the thief's motorcycle.[6]

In the case of theft attempts, individuals are advised to comply with the thief, in order to limit the chance of personal harm being done.

The U.S. Department of State also claims that,

Passengers riding in cyclos may be especially prone to thefts of personal possessions by snatch-and-grab thieves, because they ride in a semi-reclining position that readily exposes their belongings and does not allow good visibility or movement. As some cyclo drivers have reportedly kidnapped passengers and extorted money, it may be risky to hire cyclos not associated with reputable hotels or restaurants.

There have been occasional reports of incidents in which an unknown substance was used to taint drinks, leaving the victim susceptible to further criminal acts. Some expatriates have reported threats of death or physical injury related to personal business disputes.

TRAFFIC AND TRANSPORTATION CONCERNS

Crossing the street in Vietnam can be a heart-stopping experience. The curb-to-curb flow of motorcycles, cyclos and increasing numbers of cars and trucks, most of which disregard basic traffic rules, make for a symphony of chaos and plenty of close calls. Traffic lights have recently become common in the country, as the number of motorized vehicles has dramatically increased in the past 10 years, but congestion is still frenzied and chaotic. If there isn't a traffic police officer on the corner enforcing the red lights, people ignore the signals and intersections become free-for-alls.

If an expatriate is driving (or is a passenger in) a car that gets into an accident, he or she can expect to pay compensation oftentimes regardless of who was at fault. Fortunately, the compensation is usually quite reasonable. One expatriate explained, "I opened my taxi door and an oncoming motorbike slammed into it. The driver of the motorbike lost a large caldron of soup that was tied to his backseat, and had to go to the hospital to have his ear stitched up. The hospital bill amounted to about $20 and the compensation for the lost soup, $15. The driver of the taxi asked for $60 to fix the dent in his door. The police never got involved."

Own a reliable automobile and hire a good driver to navigate the streets for you; you will get to your destination unscathed and with your wallet intact. It is unwise to drive a motorbike in Vietnam. While a motorbike can be more convenient than a car for ease of parking and agility on the packed streets, surrounding oneself in reinforced steel is recommended for Vietnam's hectic traffic. Buses are not a good option either. Understanding the system is difficult for a non-Vietnamese speaker, the buses are not well-kept, and the occasional pick-pocket targets unsuspecting bus riders.

SOCIAL, CULTURAL AND RECREATION OUTLETS

While there are a number of social and recreational activities available in both Hanoi and Ho Chi Minh City, most are geared towards the local population, and there are some challenges especially for families with children. The weather often makes it difficult to spend much of the day outside, and because the sidewalks are used for parking motor bikes, it is very difficult to use a pram or stroller in the cities. Movie theaters dub the films in Vietnamese, so for English speakers the movie-going experience can be disappointing.

Shopping is a fun activity especially for furniture and house wares, but buying clothing can be challenging if you are a Westerner because very few retail outlets carry Western-sized clothing. However, tailoring is an option for larger-sized women and men.

You will not go hungry or thirsty in either Ho Chi Minh City or Hanoi, as there are many excellent restaurants and bars. Local Vietnamese food has gained global popularity, and the second favorite cuisine in Vietnam is French fare.

Hanoi

Expatriates can explore the famous temples and pagodas, such as the Temple of Literature, the Jade Mountain Temple, and the One-Pillar Pagoda, as well as Ho Chi Minh's mausoleum and former residence. Hanoi does have several art and history museums, art galleries and an excellent water puppet theatre. The zoo should be previewed before bringing children, as the animals' living conditions can seem quite meager to visitors from countries with higher standards.

Another source of entertainment is the Hanoi Opera House, which is home to the Hanoi Symphony Orchestra.

Hanoi has some beautiful lakes, including Hoan Kiem Lake, Truc Bach (White Silk) Lake, and West Lake. Vendors on the Red River offer boat rides, and there is a golf course at the King Island Golf Club within close driving distance of the city center. Several major hotels offer memberships for use of their swimming pools, tennis courts and health clubs.

The countryside has several resorts that require some travel to reach, but are good for long weekend trips.

Ho Chi Minh City

According to ORC Worldwide's Location Evaluation Report, Ho Chi Minh City offers historic and religious sites to visit, as well as museums—the Fine Arts, History, Revolutionary, and War Remnants museums, to name a few—art galleries, and the Municipal Theater (sometimes called the opera house). Historical places of interest include the Reunification Hall and the Cu Chi Tunnels, an underground network of tunnels extending to Cambodia that was built during the Vietnam War.

Among religious sites are the Mari Amman Hindu temple, the Saigon Central Mosque, and the Notre Dame Cathedral. Ho Chi Minh City also has botanical gardens, a zoo, and markets with a vast array of merchandise.

There are several golf courses within an hour and a half of downtown by car, as well as many tennis courts and other sports facilities.

Outside the city, beach resorts along the South China Sea offer snorkeling, diving and deep-sea fishing.

SCHOOLING

Unfortunately, corruption occurred recently at one of the few international schools in Hanoi, which affected expatriate children. As Thomson Reuters' news service reported on June 4, 2007:

> Hundreds of parents and children at an international school in Hanoi are caught in the middle of a joint venture turned sour between Vietnamese and Vietnamese-American partners. For more than a year, accusations of embezzlement, mismanagement, and lack of transparency have beset Hanoi International School in a case that diplomats say is emblematic of difficulties that sometimes mar business in Vietnam. Management issues include failure to convene a board meeting, up

to $2 million unused for school development, lack of books, and an inoperable Internet server needed by some children for exams.[7]

Fortunately for those who are assigned to Ho Chi Minh City, a wide variety of excellent, well-managed international schools are available.

Ho Chi Minh City

Language and curriculum differences make the local school system a poor match for expatriate children, who are better served in international schools. Ho Chi Minh City has a wide variety of schools available, including schools with French, Korean, Japanese, English, and American curriculums. Many of the schools are excellent, and two with longstanding, solid reputations are the International School of Ho Chi Minh City and the British International School, with main campuses in the popular An Phu district. The Saigon South International School is following the U.S. curriculum and is located in District 7, which is generally known as "Saigon South."

Hanoi

Hanoi has one primary international school for English-speaking children: The United Nations School of Hanoi. The Vietnamese Ministry of Education also provides English language education in the Hanoi International School, · as well as a French school (Lycée Français Alexandre Yersin de Hanoï) and the Japanese School of Hanoi which offers a Japanese curriculum.[8]

INFRASTRUCTURE CONCERNS

Supplies of electricity and water can be problematic; there are frequent brief power outages and fluctuations in voltage, as well as occasional water shortages. Surge protectors are recommended to protect electronic equipment. While the landline telephone system is adequate, most people prefer to use cellular phones. Postal services are adequate, albeit expensive for international post, and if a package is important, it is wise to use a courier. The banking system is adequate, but the choice of banks is limited and service tends to be slow. The city does have ATMs, but very few are connected to international banks.[9]

RELIGIOUS MATTERS

Organized religion is of great concern to the Communist Party, who treats it as if it is a threat to their authority.

According to ORC Worldwide's Location Evaluation Report,

> The Vietnamese government acts harshly toward dissidents, critics and others it considers to be subversive, including religious groups, ethnic Montagnards (from the highlands of Vietnam), and political organizations. Political opponents are routinely imprisoned.[10]

If you are religious, be careful that your place of worship has the right to assemble, as religious groups need government clearance to hold gatherings, and don't distribute bibles or other religious materials, as proselytizing is not allowed.

She is a grandmother who is married to an American man whom she met while he was serving a tour of duty in Vietnam in the 1960s. She knew how the Vietnamese government felt about the distribution of bibles to non-Christians in Vietnam, but in 2006, she knowingly gave one to an acquaintance in Ho Chi Minh City. That man turned out to be an undercover policeman, who put her in his jeep between two of his comrades and took her to the police station. He told her to leave Vietnam and not to come back, which ruined her plans to retire in Vietnam, her home country.

HOUSING

Ho Chi Minh City

Typically, expatriates live in either serviced apartments or villas, which are single-family detached houses. Serviced apartments usually have concierge services, as well as daily or weekly housekeeping included in the rental fee. Amenities for apartment blocks and villas within compounds tend to include swimming pools, workout centers, security and tennis courts. The two most popular locations for expatriate housing in Ho Chi Minh City are An Phu and Phu My Hung. There are also a number of serviced apartments in the city center, which are quite popular with expatriates.

An Phu is the more established neighborhood, while Phu My Hung is a very new development. Expatriates who travel to factories on the outskirts of Ho Chi Minh City might favor An Phu over Phu My Hung because it is located on the highway which runs out towards many of the industrial parks. However, expatriates who work in the city center (District 1) will find a faster commute from Phu My Hung.

According to ORC Worldwide, the market for housing, especially for villas in Ho Chi Minh City, is tight in areas that are favored by expatriates, which is causing increases in rental rates.

Hanoi

According to ORC Worldwide,

> Several Hanoi neighborhoods are popular with expatriates. Areas in central Hanoi include the prestigious Ba Dinh District, home to diplomatic missions and residences; Hoan Kiem District, especially near Hoan Kiem Lake; and the Tay Ho, Dong Da, and Hai Ba Trung districts. Also popular are Truc Bach; Nhai Tam/Quang Ba, near West Lake; and Lang Ha/Giang Vo and Van Phuc. Many Japanese expatriates live in Thuy Khue (Japanese Village). The Ba Dinh and Tay Ho districts have international schools.

Availability is currently limited for apartments, especially high-end ones, but houses are available, as new construction is bringing more on the market. Houses tend to be fairly large with three or more bedrooms, and they usually do not have a yard. Furnished houses are available, but most are unfurnished; most apartments are furnished.

GOODS AND SERVICES

Shoppers can find most food items in Hanoi and Ho Chi Minh City. Most fresh fruits, vegetables, fish and some meats are local, and several imported canned goods are readily available in local supermarkets. It is a good idea to check expiration dates of packaged food items and to be careful with repackaged items (such as rice and flour), as insect infestation can be a problem. In addition to the supermarkets' huge inventory, there are several local markets with a wide variety of fresh produce available. Sanitary measures are necessary when shopping for and preparing fresh food, particularly fruits, vegetables, and poultry.[11]

While the selection of good-quality clothing has improved, some expatriates still tend to buy what they need during their home visits or elsewhere abroad. While some English and other language books are available, the selection is somewhat limited.[12]

AIR TRAVEL FROM VIETNAM

Both Ho Chi Minh City and Hanoi offer direct flights to many Asian locations. There are some direct flights to Europe, but almost all flights to North America require at least one connection. Vietnam Airlines offers many domestic flights from Hanoi and Ho Chi Minh City each day, and normally the flights are on time and quite comfortable. The flight from Hanoi to Ho Chi Minh City is about two hours long.

ENDNOTES

1. "Directorate for Standards and Quality, Vietnam," http://www.tcvn.gov.vn/en/index.php
2. Vietnam National Administration of Tourism, climate information, http://vietnamtourism.com/e_pages/country/province.asp?uid=71
3. ORC Worldwide, "Location Evaluation Report for Ho Chi Minh City, Vietnam" and "Location Evaluation Report for Hanoi, Vietnam," July 2008.
4. WHO, "Country Cooperation Strategy: Vietnam 2003 – 2006," http://www.who.int/countryfocus/cooperation_strategy/ccs_vnm_en.pdf
5. Family Medical Practice, Ho Chi Minh City Branch, September 2008.
6. U.S. Department of State Vietnam Country-Specific Information, February 2008, http://travel.state.gov/travel/cis_pa_tw/cis/cis_1060.html
7. Thomson Reuters New Service, June 4, 2007.
8. ORC Worldwide, "Location Evaluation Report for Ho Chi Minh City, Vietnam" and "Location Evaluation Report for Hanoi, Vietnam," July 2008.
9. Ibid.
10. Ibid.
11. Ibid.
12. Ibid.

Index